I don't work Fridays

MARTIN NORBURY

RETHINK PRESS

First published in Great Britain 2016 by Rethink Press (www.rethinkpress.com)

Praise

"It's great, I was gripped."
JEZ ROSE, BEST SELLING AUTHOR OF *PURPLE BANANA, HAVE A CRAP DAY* AND *EXTRAORDINARY RESULTS FROM ORDINARY PEOPLE*

"Martin has a unique way of looking at things. This comes across in a book that is packed full of simple yet powerful ideas that, if applied, will put you and your business in a stronger, healthier place."
ASH TAYLOR, THE IMPLEMENTATION COACH

"The principles and philosophies of business success in a nutshell."
CLAIRE PERRY LOUISE, THE MEMBERSHIP EXPERT

"It's absolutely wow; totally resonated with me."
LUCY COLLIER, DIRECTOR OF MARKETING, THE FRANCHISE REVOLUTION

"I've read many business books, but few relate personal experience and give that experience a structure to make it relevant and straightforward to take to any business."
JOHN THOMPSON, MD, YOUR NEXT MORTGAGE

Contents

Foreword

After interviewing 2000+ business owners over five years I learned many things. The most important insight is that entrepreneurship is a journey, and it's a lot more predictable than you'd think. There are phases nearly every growing business goes through.

Every business was once a 'Startup'. It all begins with a great idea and a lot of enthusiasm. As a new business owner, you develop an offering, set up an office, hire the first staff members and secure some funding for the journey ahead.

Predictably, most businesses don't live up to the initial dream or expectations of the founder and soon that enthusiasm drops away. The business becomes a struggle and success seems to move away at the same speed that you chase it.

Over 70% of all businesses in the western world are very small and do not employ anyone. They carry on in 'survival mode'. They are satisfied if they can meet their bills and make some more on top, allowing them to live reasonably well.

Little do most people realise, their business is less than 18 months away from being a coveted 'lifestyle business' if they were to make some changes. A lifestyle business is achievable for almost anyone who's open to learning.

This sort of business provides a balance of financial rewards and creative freedom. It's engaging and challenging without being infuriating and draining and it's the key to achieving success in other areas of life too.

The classic mistake almost all business owners make is losing perspective. They get too close to their business and fail to see the real opportunity. It's easy to see how to improve someone else's business but difficult to have any perspective on your own operations.

Martin Norbury's book gives you practical ways to get perspective and move out of the struggle and into a lifestyle business. He has the ultimate credentials for being able to help you succeed in doing this – he's done it himself!

This book isn't based on academic theory. Even better, it's not written by a 30-something year-old male who doesn't have a family or overheads to consider.

This book is written by a successful entrepreneur with real life experience – business and personal.

My own book Entrepreneur Revolution is about helping

small business owners gain an entrepreneurial mind-set to help you break free and follow your dream. I don't work Fridays gives you a structure and set of rules to achieve this.

In my latest book, Oversubscribed, I share my recipe for ensuring demand outstrips supply for a product or service, and having scores of customers lining up to hand over their money. In this book, Martin explains the importance of alignment and getting the right team, processes and systems in place, without which your business will fail to meet this demand. He demonstrates his expertise in translating 'big business' thinking and applying it to small and medium-sized companies.

What you have in your hands is Martin's journey of discovering the key to serious business growth, interwoven with bite-sized tips on how to apply this to your business. The immense value is in the understanding and structured application of the SCALE model that Martin describes.

When Martin took part in my Key Person of Influence growth accelerator program, I used to wonder why he wasn't all that keen on committing his Fridays. I now know why. And I can see this book sparking a movement of business owners who can and do take Friday off!

Daniel Priestley

Entrepreneur and Author (*Key Person of Influence*, *Entrepreneur Revolution* and *Oversubscribed*)

Introduction

Are some people just born lucky or naturally brilliant?

I've never been much of a 'people' person – although I am a person who understands a lot about people.

Just like all of the other discoveries that we are going to explore through the pages of this book, that was something I learned much later on in my journey. It was only by looking back and getting under the surface of those experiences, that the 'Scale' philosophy for creating and managing business growth ever saw the light of day. The process was there but it needed defining in order to release its potential and turn it into something I could share.

It is an interesting observation, and far more common than you'd imagine, that successful people often don't know how they got there. Many of the pioneers, gold-medallists, award winners and multi-millionaires of our world simply can't understand why other people aren't like them. Often it is only by soul-searching and self-examination that they can even start to get a handle on what they do differently. Typically it is only when other people start studying their seemingly super-human instinct and passion that the rest of us can learn the processes and motivations that make them tick. So, if many of the greatest people who ever lived can't tell you what makes them so different, it seems logical to conclude that they genuinely were just lucky enough to be built that way.

If that is true, then life is pretty unfair, although nobody ever said that it was supposed to be fair!

The really exciting news is that those inbuilt, instinctive behaviours that drive the great and the good to live amazing lives can become learned behaviours for anyone.

The same goes for successful businesses and their owners. If you have that spark which led you to go out on your own and chase the dream, or even if you were led there through circumstance and necessity, you are already half way to escaping the norm. That is a partial compliment, but it is mainly meant as an encouragement. You see, no one ever won a race by doing really well at the beginning but not finishing. Likewise, the business that shows potential then fades away or barely touches the surface of average is as far from the headlines as it is a healthy bottom line, but if you have started and you still believe the dream is achievable, then I salute your courage and your quest for a solution. If you keep on reading, I promise to show you the 'how' which will reward the 'why' you started in the first place.

The fact is that we can all be better than we were yesterday and the cumulative effect of daily progression, applied throughout the rest of your life, would make more difference than you could possibly imagine – for you and ultimately for those that mean the most to you. Think about that for a while.

The very same principles and rules that drive excellence in 'above average' individuals can be applied to businesses. This book has been written to teach you how to apply scaling to your business, through the lessons that I have observed and learned through a life of dance, magic, rebellion, tragedy, entrepreneurship and major corporate directorship.

It is simple, it is repeatable and it is proven to work at pretty much every level of business.

The story you are about to read will take you on a journey from Cha-Cha-Cha and 'Just like that' through cocktail bars and bodyshops, visiting successful start-ups and multi-million pound rescues, to family tragedy and heartache, before descending gently on the practical 'how-to' for you.

Its retelling has been carefully structured to show the steps needed to take your business from where it is now into multiples of profit. So look out for the lessons and examples along the way, and don't worry if you miss any as I'll do a full recap at the end.

I will make no apologies for using my story as the illustration. Benjamin Franklin was right when he said:

'Tell me and I forget. Teach me and I remember. Involve me and I learn.'

Finally, why is it called 'I don't work Fridays'? You will have to read on to find out.

Part 1
I don't work Fridays...

Chapter 1
Last things first

It was a clear, bright Friday morning early in 2015. Although the sky was a stunning blue and the sun was shining, there was a bit of a frost in the air, some of which had settled gently on the windscreen, leaving pretty, crystallised shapes that needed to be removed in order to clear my vision before we set off. As I rhythmically scraped the ice away, noticing the pattern in its formation, a warm smile found its way to my mouth, the George Baker Selection's 'Paloma Blanca' entered my mind, and a little cha-cha-cha escaped through my feet. It was going to be a good day and we were just setting off to sign on the dotted line for the biggest deal of my self-employed life.

Yes – I did say it was a Friday morning and you are right, I don't work Fridays, but that is what makes this such a powerful part of the story and indeed the entire scale message. A few months earlier I'd had a chance meeting with an old business colleague of mine, while sitting on a panel of business growth experts at an entrepreneurial event. Actually,

I had seen the name of an old work colleague 'Joe' on the candidates list earlier in the day and briefly wondered if it was the same person that I hadn't seen for over a decade. So you can imagine my delight when Joe walked up to me with the sort of smile that you only get when a flood of good memories is tinged with that feeling of getting older. We caught up briefly about the old days and talked mostly about where we were now, families, colleagues we still knew and business.

When I had known Joe previously he had run an independent bodyshop as part of a larger organisation in which I was involved. The Edenbridge Accident Repair Centre had evolved into a fully managed service for customers, designed to deal with every aspect of their need after an accident, from the claim through to the repair. He explained to me how he had realised that the inward looking attitude of the motor industry had meant they had lost sight of customers' actual needs. This had driven him to change the focus and build his business from the customer requirement upwards.

As you will learn when I go deeper into my story, I had a history in the motor trade and had even had a little bit of influence from time to time. I'd helped make changes before and still knew some of the key players at the top, so the seed of an idea began to form in both our minds.

The question that Joe and I couldn't get out of our heads was that if he had managed to build a successful business by putting customers first – and the rest of the industry was struggling by chasing the pound – how could we go about changing an entire industry? We kept in touch and played with a few ideas, eventually hatching a plan to create the perfect solution by taking Joe's model and amplifying it using the scale philosophy that I will be describing to you in this book.

So on this particular Friday morning (I remember it well because Diana Ross's 'Chain Reaction' came on the radio just as I got on the motorway to head to London) the sharp, sunny brightness seemed to set the scene perfectly. It felt a bit like the final piece in a chain reaction, coming full circle back to one of the biggest influences of my working life, to start talking about multi-million pound deals once more.

In short we needed £200 million to get our plan off of the ground and revolutionise the accident management and repair industry. With this money we planned to buy £1 billion of turnover and scale it into an efficient, customer focused model that would perpetuate growth and efficiency. We had built the model, proved it would work and were on our way to demonstrate the credibility and certainty of our plan. We had garnered a lot of interest to raise £49 million of backing and the people we were about to meet in the city were the key to raising the remainder.

Of course we were nervous, but it was more of an excitement built on confidence in a process in which we believed, and could prove.

The irony of the meeting being held on a Friday didn't escape me, although it did feel a little odd getting dressed for work rather than play that morning. By then it had been many years since I had given up some of my precious Friday family time to do any work, but today I had chosen to, which is why it was OK. In all truth I could have changed the meeting to any day I wanted but, while my initial reaction had been to do just that, it seemed somehow appropriate to make this the exception.

The rest of this book will explain why I don't work on Fridays and, more importantly, how I have put myself in a position to be able to make that choice each week.

Chapter 2

Setting the scene for scale

Being able to scale your business gives you access to a whole manner of exciting and new opportunities and possibilities. I will share with you, the lifetime of learning and discovery that led me to this point and how I discovered scale. I could just teach you my method, but one of the things I have learned is that discovery is a far more powerful teacher than simply being told.

So as I retell my story I challenge you to:

- Make notes in the spaces provided at the end of each chapter
- See if you can discover what scale means from the clues in the stories
- Read, study and then give this book to someone else who you think would benefit from it.
- Go to http://myadvocatementor.com/books/ for templates and exercises
- Follow us on Twitter *@DontWork_Friday* and Like us on Facebook *I don't work Fridays* to share stories of your discoveries #idontworkfridays

For me it was an informal comment, made by fellow (and highly successful) entrepreneur Kate during a business mastermind meeting in 2013, that stopped me in my tracks and made me look at myself and what I actually wanted. She simply said, 'You are my scalability coach' and carried on talking to another member of the group. I have to be honest and say that I remember little else of that meeting. Instead my mind began racing back and forth across the decades of my life, briefly landing on key moments of clarity before shooting off to find the next – recalling and identifying all the major milestones where I had learned how to scale. Over the next few weeks as I began to set out these lessons in order and draw out the processes hidden within them, a pattern began to emerge.

'You are my scalability coach.'

It was as clear as the moment when a mass of bodies in a dance troupe suddenly emerges in perfect order, rhythm and step, to gracefully and dramatically close the show. I had finally discovered the process that I had unknowingly been using since my childhood to forge a path through life, challenge the norm and win more often than I lost for over forty years.

I had uncovered my secret of scale: could it help others? At the end of this book I will share the formula, successes and some of the practical detail that will enable you to scale your business and then sack yourself (if you choose to). You could turn there now, but that would be a mistake because, like anything else in life, the power is in the detail, the discovery of it and the way that is applied in real life.

These principles and the processes that I developed have helped me learn how to entertain a crowd, deal with life and the tragedy it sometimes hands out, start up, grow and sell my own business, turn loss-making multi-million pound corporates into profitable success stories and, latterly, work with clients from over thirty different business sectors, showing them how to scale their own businesses.

One of my biggest 'learns' and in many ways the one that underpins the scale philosophy and everything else I have achieved and seen other people achieve, is that life is a really a big game. It is massively important and the stakes couldn't be higher, but it is a game nonetheless: a game like any other, which you are far more likely to win if you understand its aim and associated rules, strategies and structures. What would happen if you knew the rules so well that you could manipulate them to suit your purpose? What if you could learn how to observe what was going on around you and write the rule book yourself? Surely that would give you the absolute advantage. Surely that would show you the route to winning the game – on your terms.

Now I am not claiming to have played the game with absolute mastery from day one. True mastery comes from understanding why things work the way that they do. For the most part I simply followed my instinct, made fast decisions, fought the 'accepted' system a little bit, and became comfortable outside my comfort zone. As time went on I observed, learnt from my mistakes and my successes, and as I progressed from one stage of my life to the next, I began to see that the rules were always the same. It was simply that the application of them needed to be re-written to best suit each new scenario.

Part 2
Unconscious Scale

Chapter 3
Discoveries on the dance floor

My first true contact with rules and process started with ballroom dancing (long before it was strictly fashionable). It was 1975 and I was just eight years old – an impressionable age where the very last thing that you would want to be was 'different'. We were living in Wexham, Slough – me, my parents and my sister Cheryl, who was six years older than me and equally keen not to be embarrassed by her younger brother. Cheryl regularly attended ballroom dancing lessons, which for girls in the 1970s was an acceptable hobby or pastime, possibly even a very cool one.

So to avoid any embarrassment or distraction, I stayed at home under the watchful eye of our next door neighbour (an off-duty policeman), dreaming about the day I would walk out onto the hallowed Anfield turf and score a hat trick in front of The Kop. One particular Sunday, my babysitter was called out to a police emergency – which left little other option than for me to tag (or as I recall, be dragged) along to the dance hall and watch my ever-so-slightly embarrassed sister learn to dance. To be honest, I don't really remember much about that first visit but it seems that I responded to the offer to have a go myself. I have also since been informed that my reaction after the event was really positive, and that I asked to go back the next week and the next. I'm not exactly sure what it was about dancing that got under my skin either, but before very long at all I was completely hooked.

For me it was just one of those difficult things which came really easy. I knew it was hard by the reaction of most of the other students in the class to the continual, repetitive nature of learning the steps, breaking down each movement and perfecting its intricacies over and over and over again, but I found that it was highly addictive and easy.

LESSON TO LEARN

Natural talent alone will rarely be enough to get anyone to their goals. You need to work really hard to achieve anything in life. When I talk to my clients today, business owners and entrepreneurs, I always start with trying to understand 'why' they started in the first place. Some are able to give a direct answer straight away and relay their very clear goals, ambitions and tropical island retirement plans, but most talk around the edges of the start of their journey, drift off a little into the immediate future for a while and then arrive back at simply enjoying the work that they do. These people are the ones that I can help the most, but only if they are prepared to accept that desire alone will not get them to where they want to be.

It was the same when I discovered a love of dancing and awoke my natural passion for its movement, energy and musicality – I would only become the best through guidance, discipline, routine and hard work. Without those outside influences and internal qualities the passion would never have become anything more than a hobby.

I carried on dancing until I was fifteen years old, and while my introduction to it had been a result of happenstance fuelled by an untapped appetite, the way I became one of the best was a long way from serendipity.

My favourite dance was the Cha-Cha-Cha, overflowing with its colourful Latin flavours, but defined by the energy and steady beat of its repeating steps and stylish flair. I loved the performance but became obsessed with practising the moves over and over again until I had achieved perfection. In direct contrast to my increasingly unlikely chance of a football career, dance put me in total control of my potential. Whereas the thrill of kicking a ball around the playground lay in its uncertainty, ever-changing positions and possibilities, dance was totally predictable. It still delivered the greatest buzz of energy, adrenalin and excitement that my short life had ever known, but it was ordered, it had a plan, and I was perfecting my part.

Although I didn't know it at the time (I was just having fun) I had stumbled across the world-beating power of setting up a system, laying out a path to success, and repeating it over and over again until it was flawless.

Looking back, I can see that this process of learning the basic steps of ballroom dancing and understanding the fundamental movements required was setting me up to become a very good dancer. It was like I was becoming familiar with the basic rules of the game and putting myself in a place where I could control them.

As you can imagine, it wasn't easy being a dancer at that age, in those days (just ask Billy Elliot), but like so many of the most valuable things in life, the cost was incomparable to the benefits. I chose not to tell my friends at school; so it became my secret double-life, I was good at it, and it was filling my veins with confidence. Not just in terms of the sheer thrill of being on the dance floor, or the pure joy of performing a perfect routine or winning a competition, but because the people who I trusted around me were impressed. This, I was later to discover, was also an important factor in my development of the scale philosophy – the need for feedback and appreciation. A report in the local paper, declaring my victory in a major dance competition soon spoiled my dance anonymity, especially when the headmaster spotted the article and highlighted it to the entire school one assembly. It's those sort of experiences that toughen you up in life.

At one of our local party dances, a senior figure in the dancing world at the time (long before he was praising celebrities on national TV for floating across the dance floor like butter on a crumpet), a man by the name of Len Goodman, was visiting the dance club as an adjudicator and mentioned to my local tutor (Bill) that he could see some potential. He suggested getting me a permanent partner, an outfit, some better dance shoes and entering me into some competitions. So Martin and Julie (my new dance partner) became the next stage of my dance journey. It wasn't too long after that my local dance schoolteacher, Bill Phillips, set his sights on a pretty big target for us. The 8-to-10 Cha-Cha-Cha was being held in Bognor Regis in the spring of 1977, at which Bill was invited to present the trophy to the winners. Bill had set his sights on getting us ready to enter and win the most prestigious title available for our age group.

Fortunately Julie shared my passion for following the system that we were being taught and the congruency of our work ethic was delivering the result that we, and Bill, desired. The mirror became our best friend, and we learned not only how to dance better but to listen to our teacher's corrections. We practiced as they slowly pointed our technique towards perfection. Over and over and over again, going through the steps, converting expert tuition into muscle memory and what the plan dictated, into the reality that the mirror reflected. It was hard work, but I loved it. At times I just wanted to move on to something else, but I knew that what I was doing would get me the result that I coveted more than anything else in the world at that time. We had lessons and/or practiced every day, including weekends, apart from Fridays which was not possible because of my parents work commitments (even then I didn't work Fridays).

My passion had found the process to set it up for the end goal – and I had absolute clarity about the way that Julie and I would get there.

LESSON TO LEARN

When you get to the top level in dance, the medals are decided based on performance, flair and precision – getting the basics right is a given. Today in business we might refer to that as marginal gains, USPs or differentiators, which make one company, stand apart from its competition, but too many companies fail because they are obsessed with the extras and stop paying attention to the basics. It is as if they are trying to finish the journey too early and reach their peak before they have steadied the ship. They stop paying attention to the basic functions of the business and the people that are at the heart of it – their employees. As many dancers have found to their detriment over the years, a lack of attention to the basics can result in a short and largely unsuccessful career – it is no different for a business.

You see, it is the basics that give a business its strength. It is the regular monitoring or gradual improvement of the fundamental processes, which provide its efficiency and profitability. Only when people know what the correct process looks like, and there is a way of tracking that this pattern is followed, can the business start to grow safely. Only then can it truly start to realise its potential.

It is the perfecting of the basics that becomes the foundation for a world championship dance routine. The endless hours of rehearsing and correcting the intricacies of each step until you know what perfect 'feels' like are irreplaceable. Then, when it comes to adding the finesse, and focusing on the performance it really is very easy. 100% has become the most natural thing in the world, a level at which you can perform with ease and without fail. Setting up the foundation principles correctly makes all the difference in the push for excellence. So from that systematic mastery of the technique, Julie and I were able to add our own style, personality and flair to our championship routine.

And that is how we won the 8-to-10 Cha-Cha-Cha in April 1977.

The competition was akin to the best newcomers at the Oscars as many winners and finalists went on to become the world champions of the future. It was also widely recognised that the trophy was bigger than the average ten-year-old!

If dance was a passion and a labour of love as represented by the 'rat-ta-tat-tat tat-' of The Manhattan Transfer's 1977 hit 'Chanson D'Amour', then my school days were more akin to angst epitomised by the Jam and their classic hit 'Eton Rifles': 'There's a row going on down near Slough…'

Chapter 4

The lessons and anti-lessons of education

I was born in Wexham, Slough in 1967 and grew up in a small house with my parents and older sister. Dad worked for the council, running logistics for the Sewerage Department, from where he moved into the private sector, working for a pharmaceutical company, and eventually bought the council house we were living in. So having seen my family make the move from working class towards middle class my 'handed down' aspiration was to always stay there. Bigger ambitions only came into play as I learned that to most of the people I grew up with, becoming like your parents was the norm. I eventually learnt that following in my father's footsteps wasn't the right path for me.

My first school in 1972 was Eton Wick Church of England Junior School and one of my earliest memories was being the second kid in my year to be able to read. I have no idea where

Robert is today, but he will forever hold the honour of top spot over me. I suppose that for me to remember that particular detail it must have meant a lot to me at the time.

Shortly after settling in, we moved house and I joined Wexham Junior School. There I discovered that the early accolade for reading was an indicator that 'learning' was going to be one of my strengths (when I chose to apply myself). That in itself threw up a few challenges and made for some fairly tough learning experiences at such a young age.

When it came to study, in many ways in total contrast to the work ethic of my dancing experience (which was happening at the same time), I found that I was simply able to consume the information and pass the tests. So when the Eleven Plus examinations came round in 1978 it was just me and two other boys from the school who passed and were able to go on to grammar school. On the face of it this should have been a good thing, but in reality it meant a fair bit of exclusion within the neighbourhood; many of my former school friends, possibly under the influence of their parents, never spoke to me again. The regular thing was to go to the state senior school down the road and by qualifying to attend grammar school, I had unwittingly put myself outside of the crowd (another great lesson).

So in 1979 I started a new stage of my life at Slough Grammar School, which was an all-boys school with around eighty students in my year, made up of four classes of twenty odd (literally in some cases) boys. It was here that I learned another three really important lessons that would eventually become a fundamental part of the scale philosophy that I was inadvertently uncovering.

The first of these major learns was that confidence could cross boundaries and be applied in different scenarios to quite significant effect. By this time I had been dancing for four or five years, the 8-to-10 Cha-Cha-Cha was under my belt along with many other awards – and for my age and category I had reached the rank of being in the Top Four for any competition we entered. The huge amount of self-confidence that I got from dancing meant that, while I knew no one in the grammar school when I arrived, I was very quickly and easily able to find my place and make new friends. I suppose I had developed a habit of winning and the belief of being good at whatever I put my hand, feet or mind to – when I tried, that was. So without really knowing how, or having a strategy to get me there, I had reapplied the same dancing self-belief to my social circumstances. Blondie was in the charts singing 'Heart of Glass' the year I arrived at Slough Grammar School and I was determined that mine wouldn't be shattered by the experience.

LESSON TO LEARN

Confidence in business, just as in life, is an artificial emotion. While it is true that external environments can contribute to the feeling of being capable and worthy of surviving or excelling in a particular scenario, it is what is inside of an individual that determines their approach. For me, as I started grammar school, I had every right to feel nervous and have a degree of doubt about my justification for being there. I had grown up living on a council estate and arrived as another student from a large state school that had just made himself a virtual outcast by being successful in an end of year test. On my first day I only knew two other boys, and even those were only really 'know by sight and name' relationships, but I simply took an area of my life where I knew I was a success (clearly I didn't even know at the time that I was using this technique) and inserted that into my new situation.

If you are in business, then it must be because you are good at something. For most it started with the feeling that, 'I could do that much better than other people are doing it' or perhaps the belief that your expertise and passion for your dream could turn you into a success one day. Whatever the source of your confidence you can use the same power elsewhere. When you understand that confidence is simply the result of a process, which you control, then you are in charge of the game and its rules. To say confidence is all in the mind might be a little bit too general – but it is definitely a part of you, not a result of what happens around you. The key is to find yours and learn how to use it well in a multiple of scenarios.

This sense of being sure of my own character and ability really came into its own after a few months when the local council took the decision to merge the town's boys and girls schools into one. To most of my mates this could not have been worse news – who wanted these strange creatures called 'girls' getting in the way of our boyish larks? In truth though, we were simply at that age where most boys were a little intimidated by a pretty girl, but for me it was different again. I had been dancing with girls since I was seven and this news was music, rhythm and sway to my ears, but it also represented a whole new world full of distraction, which in the end spelled the demise of my quest for an education. Within a few years I had been expelled or, as Mum put it, 'The headmaster saw your aspirations differently'. That's why we love our mums.

I'll come back to that story shortly, but first let me share the second big lesson about the scale principle which life at Slough Grammar School taught me. The whole point of attending one of the top ten grammar schools in the country was so that I could go to Oxford or Cambridge at the end of it. My parents really wanted me to enter into a law career, and I also liked the idea. So I was working towards getting a good grade in what we referred to as the 'Oxbridge Exam'. All the predictions prior to my eventual expulsion suggested that I could sail through, if I applied myself, but even before the distracting and destructive presence of girls was introduced to the equation, I made another discovery which should have been good news but would come back to haunt me many more times. I worked out that I could successfully cram (study hard at the last minute) and get away with it.

This revelation came during a school cricket match one lovely, warm summer day. I was due to sit a history exam the following morning and I wanted to spend some time in the sunshine; so I took my pink book with me (each subject was colour coded and for some reason history was pink) and I made myself comfortable. For the entire match I simply read the relevant information and crammed my head full of dates, victories and various world-changing acts of intrigue or valour – all to the background of ball thudding on bat, occasional rounds of polite applause and a few cries of, 'howzat!'. As I recall, it was a very pleasant afternoon indeed. The next day, I turned up at the exam, full of my usual confidence but also fully aware that I was more than a little unprepared. But it seemed to go OK and to my utter amazement I ended up scoring the top marks for the entire year.

This taught me a kind of anti-lesson in that I realised that I could get away with a degree of success without putting in too much effort. Ask any fifteen year old today if they would like to be in that position and they would jump at the opportunity, but I call it an anti-lesson because it could quite easily have become my downfall.

LESSON TO LEARN

Many businesses today are able to survive on talent and talent alone, but all they can ever do is just survive. These are the ones that do a good job, have a reasonably good reputation in their particular marketplace, can get by in a variety of disciplines, and are generally a good company to use (from a customer's perspective) but they never get bigger than 'average'. They exist on fumes from their cash flow, they run around like crazy tending to customer whims, and they spend a lot of time wrestling with their bottom line. The reality is that these businesses cannot grow because they do not have the processes and disciplines in place to create a scalable business model. They have not Set up their goals and targets; there is no unity of vision; they do not have measurements in place or a way of improvement by learning lessons; and their exit plan is simply, 'more of the same'. To grow a business successfully you need to let the system deliver the excellent result – not the people.

The cricket match experience had shown me that it was possible to take the easy route to a successful result. What it didn't tell me was that quick wins were not a sustainable plan for a successful life. The confidence I had gained from dancing showed me that I could apply a strong quality that was inside of me to a number of different scenarios, but it didn't prepare me for the result of misapplying my confidence and letting its short term benefits distract me from my bigger goals.

I was sixteen years old, Mum and Dad had just finalised a divorce, which had been many turbulent years in the making, and I was fighting a multitude of emotional, educational and aspirational battles. Within a year, as a direct result of my disruptive approach to learning and my inclination to spend my time talking to the girls, I had been expelled. As far as my education was concerned, The Human League's iconic 1982 hit, 'Don't You Want Me' captured my cry towards the hand that life had dealt me.

The next three or four years of my life were a whirlwind of adolescent selfishness and disruptive drifting. I got involved in all sorts of horrible things, most of which I'm not proud of, and I generally did my own thing regardless of anyone else. I'd gone from naturally not fitting in to being determined not to. Then, through a chance conversation with one of my friends, I heard that a girl I really liked (Sarah) was going to Windsor College – so I found out which course she was doing and enrolled. Crazy really – but it suited my goals at the time (plus they had table-football in the common room). That venture didn't last very long and, while it was a lot of fun, it eventually signalled the end of my up and down attempt at education. But what a lot of valuable scalability techniques it had taught me!

LESSON TO LEARN

Not that I would ever encourage missing out on an education (if it is an essential route to your chosen goal) but there is quite a fanfare of famous business people who dropped out of the education system early to go on to big things. These include: Sir Richard Branson, Henry Ford, Walt Disney, Andrew Carnegie and Ingvar Kamprad.

'Thinking is the hardest work to do, that's
why so few people are engaged in it.'

HENRY FORD

The third and most obvious lesson from my time at Slough Grammar School was hidden in plain view. Our school motto was *Ad Astra*, a Latin phrase meaning 'To the Stars'. This was core to everything that the school stood for and my habits over the five plus years I was 'attending': how we approached our lessons; what our ambitions were; our attitude; everything. My roots were from an average council estate – what right did I have to desire to go to Oxford? But from day one, I started to not only dream but also believe that I not only could but should go there. I firmly put this down to our school motto and the higher standards, against which I started to judge myself.

It will come as no surprise that still to this day that motto is a major part of my life and it's our company motto. So what's yours?

Chapter 5

Magic secrets and cocktail flair (aka Cooper and Cruise)

During the latter years in the decline of my education, I re-engaged with an earlier passion for magic. My parents had given me a magic set for Christmas in 1976 and it had caught my imagination for exploring the potential within the impossible. For someone whose obsessions up to the time I left school exposed flair, the capacity to learn complex processes and more than a little tendency towards mischief, it was only natural that magic would attract my eye. David Cooper, brother of the incomparable Tommy Cooper, owned a magic shop on Slough High Street, adjacent to Slough Grammar School, and the lure was too much for me to resist. I dug out the magic set I'd had as a child, practised a few of the tricks to the point of perfection, and went over to the store to show off my talents.

I don't know if it was my dance confidence coming out again or if the practice really paid off (maybe it was a combination of the two) but I soon landed myself a Saturday job demonstrating new tricks to customers in the shop. I was in my element, but once again it was only looking back, years later, that I started to see the value of what these episodes in my life were teaching me. My favourite trick, and one I still like to entertain my children (and anyone else in the vicinity) with today, was the magic paddles illusion. It was the ultimate misdirection and sleight of mind, involving two small paddles where dots appear to jump from one paddle to another. It was and still is a delight to perform, a puzzle to watch, and one of those things which, even when you know the secret, will dazzle any spectator's senses. I often think that, if there really was such a thing as magic, a well-performed paddles routine is what it would look like. The concept of magic tricks, like that represented by the paddles illusion, is astoundingly precise when used as an analogy for scaling a business.

Like so many great magic tricks, the secret is simple enough to be hidden in plain sight, but subtle enough to escape the attention of the casual observer; another *Ad Astra* moment. The effect is startling and impressive, and creates wonder and curiosity. The reaction from most people is to feel that the performer is either incredibly talented with super-human speed, or that it really is genuine magic. Whichever response the spectator gravitates towards, and whether they are impressed or annoyed by the remarkable display they have just witnessed, they will inevitably decide that it would be impossible for them to duplicate the effect. They are of course wrong.

Tommy didn't come into the shop very often (by then he was not a well man) but when he did you could tell there was something naturally great within him. He was a phenomenon, a unique talent, and someone who perfectly fitted the bill for his time. When people talk of Tommy Cooper the phrases that you usually hear are things like 'comic-genius' and 'legend' (or as Tommy would say leg-end), but in all truth the act shouldn't really have worked.

He was an incredibly awkward looking man at 6 feet 4 inches high, with an array of scruffy hair and a range of graceless physical movements. Most of the magic that he performed either exposed the secret behind the trick or simply went wrong – often horribly. His off-screen life was littered with scandal, rumour and tales of depression and alcoholism. Even the jokes he told were of the very simplest sort – the kind of things that you might hear being giggled over by boys in a junior school playground.

And yet he is remembered as the stand-out comedian of his generation. A consummate performer who came to life on stage and had his audience rolling in the aisles, often before he had even said a word. I cannot claim to have known him, but I am absolutely certain of one thing. All of his bumbling and fumbling, his mistakes, his forgetfulness and his ungainly attire and appearance were done on purpose. His act may have been laced with spontaneity and he was undoubtedly adept at reacting to the whims of his adoring audience, but he performed in a way that he knew they were going to love. He had adapted and adopted the things that had worked the best for him over many years. From his days serving as an Entertainments National Service Association comedian during the Second World War, when he first learned that tricks going wrong was funny; through to his chance encounter with what was to become his trade-mark Fez, he simply learned what worked and built it into his act. Tommy Cooper was building his repertoire and reputation by just doing more of what his audience demanded. He scaled ordinary talent into legend status by hard work and attention to detail.

LESSON TO LEARN

This is exactly the same as when average business owners come across a well structured, carefully managed and precisely executed business producing outstanding results. They look in awe at the healthy, growing, over-achieving spectacle in front of them and assume that there is something magical, incredibly lucky or at best unobtainable going on behind the scenes. These initial thoughts quickly move on to jealousy, snobbery or feigned disinterest because they are frustrated at not knowing 'how' it works. It is human nature to want to believe that there is always a complex secret behind any visual success.

In reality, all that the efficient business has done is apply some rules, some discipline and a way of practicing those rules until it becomes a perfectly executed magic trick. The illusion is the seemingly effortless way in which a business is able to grow in both size and profitability. The secret is a brilliant system operating in the background that has been carefully planned and Set up, shared harmoniously throughout the business, designed with alerts and lessons in place to slowly perfect the process, and simply waiting for the final curtain to come down on a fabulously successful performance – the owner's exit plan.

The other area of my early life where I saw the result of hours and hours of painstakingly repetitive practice turn into a skill that was the envy of all of my friends was cocktail flair. The year was 1987 and I was working behind a bar called The Long Island Exchange. It was a cocktail bar full of young 80s people, and I had started to learn a bit of bartending 'flair' which is the art of juggling bottles, cocktail shakers and anything else around the bar to entertain customers while making their drinks. The manager sent me on a 10-week structured flair course run by a guy called Bas Basian, a real genius and innovator of the art who subsequently worked with Tom Cruise on the set of the 1988 film *Cocktail*. In a sense this was another type of magic for me. It was a skill that I had learned and which would attract attention and impress people, but which in reality was really nothing more than determination, attention to detail, correcting mistakes and hours and hours of dedicated practice.

One evening, my performance behind the bar was spotted by Andrew Ridgeley (of Wham! fame), who invited me to go and work in his new bar, 92's Bar and Brasserie, which provided a more glamorous stage for the 'outward performance' of my 'behind the scenes' commitment to perfection.

People would often say to me that I must have lightening reflexes, fast hands, or really good eye-to-hand coordination, always with an undertone of 'I wish I could do that'. Even now it still amazes me that people are so fast to assume natural talent and rarely consider that it might just be hard work and commitment. I mean, if Tom Cruise can make it look good…

Once again I simply had a goal (to impress girls) and the desire to achieve it. There was a process that needed to be learned, practised and corrected – juggling and sleight of hand – and then there was the fun bit of putting into action the things I had perfected behind the scenes. Just as with learning to perform magic, my short time as a cocktail flair bartender taught me that most people are not prepared to discover the most effective process for getting the best results. Most people just want the shortcut – and that rarely works in the long run.

LESSON TO LEARN

What is really important when applying the idea of 'practice makes perfect' in a business environment is that you need to be practising 'perfect' things. That is why being able to identify what 100% looks like, and amend anything that falls short of that mark is so important, because once you have Set up the goals that you are trying to achieve and shared the vision with the people you are trying to achieve it with, you need to make sure the actions are effective. Often the only way to achieve this is trial and error. When I was working at The Long Island Exchange I am proud to say that, while serving customers, I never dropped a bottle (we didn't have rubber mats, just stone floors). It simply never happened, but in the hours before we opened the doors, and in my bedroom at home, there were many times that I made mistakes, which were quite often to the sounds of breaking glass and vanishing vodka.

When you are developing, systemising and streamlining the processes behind the product that you are delivering to your customers, you are going to make mistakes. The important thing is to learn from the mistake, find a way to remove or manage it, and then (this is the massive learn) ensure that it is highlighted if it happens again. If you do not have alerts in place to tell you that there is a problem in the system, then you will never get your business to a place where it can bring you perfectly executed results.

I eventually moved on from dancing, magic and cocktails, but the discipline that I learned in those extravagant pastimes and the buzz that I got from being able to perform ordinary miracles was exhilarating. The next stage of my life saw me apply the same principles and philosophies to creating business success. I suppose I was still only slightly more aware of the reason that I was doing things in this way, but I was starting to make more deliberate choices in line with applying the things that I had learned would work.

My final thought on the structured approach to delivering flair performances, and perhaps an encouragement to anyone who is still convinced that short-term effort can bring a lifetime of rewards, is that it never leaves you. It is now nearly thirty years since I first appeared in Coopers Magic Shop or dazzled drinkers at The Long Island Exchange and 92's, but I still find myself occasionally tossing a Coke bottle from behind my right hip and catching it with the same hand as it gently floats into view from the back of my left shoulder. It is what dancers and athletes call 'muscle memory' – once learned (maybe a little rustiness might creep in) it never leaves – and my eyes absolutely light up when I have a chance to perform some magic, particularly when I have a set of paddles in my hand.

It was these principles and how they combined with my tendency to rage against the status quo that formed my approach to working life. Ultimately it would lead to success, but there were many lessons to learn and even more rough edges to attend to before that.

I'm sure the great Entrepreneurs of our time have 'business memory', the business equivalent to 'muscle memory'. They take the same principles, themes and experiences from one successful business to another and most of the time create a new success. Is this innate skill or more about the process and practices repeated over and over again?

As Jim Rohn says:

'Success leaves clues'.

You just need to spot them.

Part 3
Subconscious Scale

Chapter 6

Just the job... as the boy becomes a man

Amidst the rebellion and distractions of my school days there had been the occasional brushes with the world of business and a couple of these really stand out as vivid memories. Like many of the other things I had experienced, I found I could excel when I put my mind to it.

On one occasion, Slough Grammar School ran a business venture project in conjunction with the Young Enterprise Scheme, and the team in which I was involved came second in the whole county. The accolade of being up there with the best was one I enjoyed and remembered.

Another similar experience was a scheme run by The Metal Box Company, which was a large corporate in the area at the time. They set up a business simulator programme during the summer holidays, at the end of my Fifth Form year, in which eight of us from the school were invited to take part. The format was that we would run a business in the morning as if we were a Board of Directors; sitting round a table making key decisions about the company. Then, in the afternoon, all the data was input into a computer, which formulated the results of the actions we had agreed. We were then given our performance figures and had another meeting to discuss what to do next. This process continued over a period of four days and the idea was that through trial, error and correction we should be able to get an understanding of what 'best practice' looked like. As I recall, I thoroughly enjoyed the whole process and, even while we were going through it, the confidence that I had learned through dance and the experience of applying a proven process held me in good stead. There were no prizes, other than the satisfaction of being able to create imaginary profit, but each student was assessed on aptitude, ability to learn and inclination to lead or follow within a group environment.

LESSON TO LEARN

My evaluation report read, 'Very unconventional, thinks differently to most people, will be very successful but not in the traditional way.' At fifteen years old I loved that; it fuelled my ego and enhanced my growing belief that I would be alright doing things my way. Once again I was misreading the reality of the situation (I thought it was a licence to wing it) but was, at the same time, storing up lessons that I would draw upon much later in life when I came to formulate the scale philosophy. Those early interactions with entrepreneurial activity became a seed that was just waiting to be watered from that time onwards.

From leaving college I eventually decided it was time to get a job and soon found myself walking into a recruitment agency with a copy of my Computer Science A-Level certificate in my hand. During the interview they asked if I knew anything about electronics and fixing computers, to which I replied, 'Yes – of course,' and proceeded to be offered a job with a company called Wordplex.

When showing me around on my first day, the reaction of Bob, the Team Leader, when I told him I didn't even know how to wire a plug, was one of stunned amazement. Fortunately, Bob was a decent bloke and I was a fast learner so before long I had developed a process that meant I was outperforming my colleagues.

Once again my success got me into trouble – but on this occasion I really don't think it was my fault. It was 1986 and well into the dawn of the computer age in businesses. The company division had a great business model of taking-in old proprietary computers, fixing the faults (they weren't that complicated back then) and then selling them on as reconditioned machines. Each of the repair centre staff had a target of completing ten computers per week and, because I was always refining my working methods, it wasn't long before I had regularly hit my target by the Wednesday – giving me two days to spare. The other side of my nature then kicked in and I became a disruptive influence amongst everyone else, rather than doing extra work. The subsequent discussions with the boss went along the lines of me suggesting a three-day week or extra money and him giving me an extremely direct 'No'.

My next move was offering to go out on the road as a field service engineer (I liked the idea of having a company car) but the rules said that you had to be twenty-nine years old to do that. I was eighteen, turning nineteen, at the time and an eleven year wait for career progression was not the kind of motivational statement that appealed to me. I remember leaving work one day and listening to Capital Radio when Colonel Abrams' one hit wonder 'Trapped', filtered through the car. So apt I thought. So I left after just eighteen months in my first proper job. Wordplex's management missed a trick that day, and I'll let a musical interlude explain why.

LESSON TO LEARN

If you have ever watched *Later with… Jools Holland* on BBC Two you might have noticed that he has a favourite question when he is interviewing musical legends. After their usually amazing performance on the show, demonstrating why they have stood the test of time in one of the most demanding and competitive industries in the world, he sits the artist or band down at a table for a chat. After talking about the new album or their reunion tour for a while he then shows them a clip of how they looked and sounded when they first set off on their decades' long journey to stardom. You can often see the emotion as it stirs in the eye of the performers when the camera returns to their table. Jools then leans over and says,

'Tell me – what would today's version of you say to that version, if you could give them one bit of advice?'

This is a brilliant question, but one which has very little practical use because of the impossibility of the scenario. It is however, something that other people can learn a great deal from – if they are paying attention.

So if I had been my boss, back then when I was working for Wordplex, this is what I would have said to me. I would have simply suggested a pay rise in return for documenting the process I had developed, and then promoted me to trainer/worker and asked me to teach the rest of the team how to double their productivity. By doing these simple things I would have been delivering to me some positive affirmation (having recognised that my personality craved that); I would have been openly rewarding over-performance (to inspire the rest of the team); and I would have scaled the productivity of my existing resource by 70% at very little additional cost. By documenting the process I would also have been redefining what 100% looked like for everyone in the business from that point onwards – a vitally important step in creating a scalable business model. Although they missed a trick, it worked out well for me because shortly after that I got a call from the big boys.

One company that supported the equipment Wordplex was selling, was looking for people who understood the computers inside out. So I was head-hunted by OAS (Office Automation Services), a subsidiary of Olivetti, to go and work for them. I was in dreamland, living at home with my Mum, driving a company car, and earning great money for my age at that time. The work was simple and it kept me out of trouble, for a few years at least. Most of my time was spent driving around, from Manchester to Cornwall, installing Olivetti computers within senior MOD officer's houses – simply because they needed to use up their budget for that year. The rest of my time I was still juggling bottles in bars – what more could you want at twenty?

It will be no surprise to you by now, I'm sure, to learn that boredom soon kicked in and I began to crave something different; something that would appeal more to my desire to be involved in the process. So I went back to basics and started working as the back office Support Manager in a small retail business called Softshop. This was right at the end of the 1980s, I was twenty-one years old driving an Astra GTE 16v –, oh yea! – , and we were well into the start of the home computer age, with companies like Atari, Commodore, Nintendo and Sega at the forefront of the gaming world. This new craze meant a self-generating demand for the products we were selling, so the company had a roaring trade in those early days, but my role was to build the office computer side of the business.

So I became an expert in software for the small business market; packaging and selling products like WordPerfect, SuperCalc and Paradox for DOS. Once again, I had found myself in a position where I could plan, learn, perfect, and then deliver a solution that would solve a problem. This time it was for customers, not my own interests, but all the same I was adding a new level of understanding to the wisdom accumulating exercise that was going on in my subconscious.

The process I developed went a little bit like this: Small businesses owners were looking for better ways to operate and increase their output, efficiency and ultimately to grow their turnover. They were aware of computers because their children played games on them at home, often waiting 30 minutes for a game to load from a cassette tape (if you are reading this and you were born after 1985, I kid you not – in fact some of you might even need to Google what a cassette tape was). But many of them, even at that stage, had no real concept that computers would have the ability to change everything for their business in the near future. Amstrad, Olivetti, IBM and others were building hardware to sell into the commercial market, but it would be the smart use of software that would really make a difference. They needed demonstration and education. So I simply went in, sat down with them and looked at their processes; and then showed them how our packages and solutions could make a difference. It was an easy sell, but a fulfilling one because I knew that I was helping my customers move their businesses forward. As a company we would then support the customers with training, ongoing updates or new products as they became available. The system was perfect: We were setting them up, helping them buy-in to the technology, teaching them lessons, being alert to their changing needs and then moving them forward. It was the perfect example of invisible problem meeting unidentified solution.

This time in my life still has to be one of the best from a working perspective. It was due in main to our manager Michael Foot (no, not that one). Mike to his friends, was a gentle and fair man who was very good at his job and earned respect rather than demanded it. My work colleagues and I had so much respect for him that we often took matters into our own hands by fronting up to other staff who took Mike's gentle approach as being soft. Of course Mike was fully capable of dealing with this himself, we just sped up their exit a little. Mike created a fantastic environment to work in. We pulled together when we needed to, to achieve the results, and relaxed a little when it was appropriate. We could often be found on a Friday spoofing for a 'full mutley run' where the loser paid for a Wimpy and bottle of Beck's for us all for picking a raindrop out of a selection on the window and then watching which one got to bottom last, with the poor loser again having to deliver the same fate. See, even then I didn't work Fridays. I'm sharing this fond memory with you to demonstrate the importance of aligning your values, team and environment. Even without you there, your employees will be weeding out those not on board, or disrupting the status quo.

My own personal success was also evident within that business, and I moved across all three of their branches from; Chalfont St Peter, to Weybridge and finally Uxbridge, building a great reputation as I went. After a while one of the company's managers bought one of the branches and began running it independently. He asked me to go and work for him, which I saw as an opportunity to become a bigger fish in a smaller pond for a while – so I moved on again.

All of this time I was still working in the cocktail bar; enjoying a double-life as a solution-generating, IT innovator during the day and a joy-bringing, drink-serving entertainer at night. But, looking back I think this is where my change in attitude was becoming evident and I began to take life a bit more seriously. I had left behind the selfish, late-teens tendencies and was starting to realise that helping others 'first' is the most rewarding thing in the long run. Both emotionally and as a business success strategy. The next episode in this journey towards identifying the fullness of the scale philosophy really confirms that very point. Being also a retail operation meant having to work every Saturday. This meant that I had one day a week off and guess what? It was a Wednesday (not a Friday)!

The branch that the manager had bought was near Gerrards Cross, and he had decided that we needed to clear out some old stock. So the instruction was to sell whatever was on the shelves, regardless of what the customer needed. All of a sudden this just didn't sit right with me. I remember the moment quite vividly, and actually quite emotionally, like it was yesterday. It was the last Friday in March 1991, Chesney Hawkes' 'The One and Only' was at the top of the charts and the light bulb just went off in my head. Selling things that don't add value or don't benefit the customer will simply not be good for business – theirs or ours. A one-time sale created a customer life that was as short-lived as Chesney's one-hit-wonder song. A successful career needed longevity. If we wanted our business to grow, we had to make our customers love what we were doing for them and supply them with products that delivered response. At the end of that day's trading I had a conversation with the owner. He simply couldn't see where I was coming from, so I left for the weekend knowing that I would not be back on Monday – I think he knew by that time too.

Chapter 7

Where entrepreneur and opportunity began to make sense

So on Monday 1st April 1991 I set up my first business using a little bit of office space lent to me by some friends of mine. Like so many people I have met since, who have ventured out into the world of self-employment, I simply thought I could do it better than the guy I was working for. Even though I sort of knew 'why', like most pioneering entrepreneurs I didn't really know 'what' I was doing, but there were a few things very clear in my head at that time and several more that had become part of my life DNA. What I knew was that customers were simply people looking for solutions, not boxes – things that would actually make their lives easier. I also knew that efficiency was a key element in making a business profitable and that as long as these two things were maintained everything else should fit into place. It was perhaps a basic perspective, but it served me well as a starting point and became a foundation to the culture that I was unintentionally developing.

The exchange rate between the pound and the dollar at the time was around two to one, so importing computers gave me a significant margin to play with and helped to start generating some early revenue. While still at Softshop I'd met a guy from DTK, a Chinese company based in London, who could get us a better deal on computer stock than the people they were previously using. For some strange reason the owner (my boss) didn't want to deal with him directly so I started importing them myself and selling them on to Softshop (even though I worked for him – go figure). He even paid me in advance for the stock. So by the time I set up on my own DTK had already started to see me as quite a significant reseller. For the first few months, I simply started talking to all of the people I had built personal rapport and trust with over the years. They wanted solutions from someone who they knew would understand and care about their needs – and that is what I did.

One of the earliest deals that I got involved in, operating under my new company (SOLFAN), came through a contact that I had made with some university students. During the summer holidays I employed a couple of university students who were associated with AIESEC (*Association internationale des étudiants en sciences économiques et commerciales*), an international educational organisation. This influential group would gather together the top achievers and upcoming brilliant young minds from all over the world, and bring them together to discuss global issues. As well as the brightest people coming through the educational systems of the world, its contributors included the French and British Prime Ministers, other major European leaders and the President of the United States. In 1993 AIESEC's annual conference was being held in Brighton, so it was also attracting major coverage across all of the UK's national press.

It was just after the first Gulf War and the events surrounding the conflict were still very high on everyone's agenda – so that was due to be a major topic of discussion. Many of the students were being asked to write up the details of the symposium, particularly the Middle East conflict agenda, and needed computers to facilitate this. Without really knowing where it would lead, I suggested to the two students working for me that I might be able to provide them with some hardware – to be honest it was little more than an off-hand comment at the time – but they didn't hear it that way. So at one of their regional meetings, when I was introduced to the president of AIESEC UK, who was organising the forthcoming international event, I got a bit of a shock. Before I knew it I was being treated like a hero and the saviour of the whole event because I was going to get these computers for them. Of course then I had to deliver, but my 'just started up a new business' budget didn't really stretch to giving away loads of very expensive equipment that I didn't even have.

LESSON TO LEARN

Sometimes in business you have to make important decisions based as much on gut feel and belief as you do on the logic that surrounds the circumstance. In many ways the AIESEC computer situation would become the single event, which gave my business the direction it was lacking, but at the time I didn't have any way of knowing that. All that I had were my foundation principles: create solutions to fulfil what your customers need and provide those solutions in a way that doesn't hurt the efficiency of supply (or your cash flow). This was my Set up position – the starting point in what would become the scale philosophy. I was already congruent with my goals and the actions I was taking were guided by the lessons I'd learned from the mistakes my previous employer made. In my experience it is when instinct meets instruction and goals interact with guidance, that great things begin to happen in a business.

So I went to DTK and offered them the opportunity to be a joint sponsor of the event with me in return for the computers I needed. They jumped at the chance to get some high profile representation in the UK market and we were off. Buoyed by the success (in truth it was a just a phone call – but it felt massive) I went off to broker a few more sponsorship deals. I now had 'hero' status to live up to and I wasn't going to let an opening like that slip. So I got Canon involved as the print sponsor and on the day I (just one-man-band me) stood there alongside Andersen Consulting (now Accenture) and ICI as the main sponsor of the AEISEC conference that year. The deal led to a front page profile in The Times newspaper and inclusion in the computer equipment supplies catalogues for all of the universities throughout the UK. So from then through to 1996 my business grew rapidly, initially as an IT supplier in the educational arena and then branching out into the businesses sector – particularly in the motor trade. All the time we were focused on the principles of understanding a customer's need and then fulfilling it in a profitable way.

LESSON TO LEARN

My business was called SOLFAN, which stands for 'Sick Of Looking For A Name', but there is a very important lesson for small business owners here. Getting your business name, strapline and logo are incredibly important. I struggled but, keen to get going, quickly came up with an acronym which thankfully worked. I've come across so many owners who spent so long procrastinating over the finer details that it meant they were slow to market.

Early in 1993 I got introduced to a car repair centre in Hayes that was looking to bring its operation in line with the ISO 9000 quality standards. That meant computerising its systems and I was asked to advise on which software would best fit their needs. My investigations led me to two lads, Richard and Simon, who had just set up a company called BodyMaster to supply the motor industry with IT solutions. Between us we put together a deal for the repair centre and

I came away with the best results I had achieved up to that point across both of my key measurement criteria. In the first instance my customer was absolutely delighted because I had provided them with a bespoke solution which exactly matched their needs – meaning they were able to obtain their ISO status. Goal number one – achieved. Secondly I looked at the deal and saw a 50% margin across both the hardware and software. The next step was an obvious one – look for more of the same. So I became the regional distributor for BodyMaster, based in Slough and covering everywhere West of London, selling IT bespoke solutions to the growing number of motor industry companies that wanted to systemise their quality processes and operations. In many ways I guess you could say that I rode my luck and met the right people at the right time – but I believe it was far more than simply luck.

LESSON TO LEARN

Here is why. From the time I went to school and learned to dance, through to my flirtation with magic and cocktail flair, and right on into my employee and early entrepreneurial experiences, there were a great many people that I met and opportunities that presented themselves to me. Not all of them have been mentioned in this book (I will use the excuse of space – but in reality it is out of embarrassment). Some of them were tempting in terms of finance and advancement, others had a more emotional appeal and some were simply ridiculous. I even started walking down a handful of the avenues they presented and a few of them set me back a pace or two. But it was only when these possibilities matched the goals that I had Set up (consciously or sub-consciously) that the possibility evolved into potential. Even then it was only when I applied myself through discipline, desire, measuring and adapting that the potential became a result. That is why I believe that luck has very little to do with long-term success. We all come across opportunities all of the time. The important thing is having clear enough goals and strong enough desire to identify and pursue the right ones. At best 'luck' is no more than the fact that you can create your own and be alert enough to spot opportunities amongst all of the noise. It is the same for coincidence. I have banned that word from my vocabulary. My days at Wordplex taught me huge lessons about cause and effect. Something happens that creates change somewhere else. The key is to track back until you find the cause to your effect. I am still amazed at the amount of business owners that do not know what causes their results and any changes in them.

It was during this time that I did my first serious work around creating a process, but even then I still didn't really understand why I was doing the things I was doing. I guess it was a combination of my experiences and that I had subconsciously learned that following and implementing a successful pattern worked. As the famous Dutch master of complete football, Johan Cruyff, once said,

'Before I was thirty, I played on instinct.
After I was thirty, I began to understand
why I did what I did.'

One of the quirky habits that I had picked up from when I first started out on my own as SOLFAN was 'desk-jumping'. The office space that I was renting had four desks and, because I was in the IT market, it seemed like a logical thing for me to set up a computer on each one – even though I was the only permanent member of staff. Depending on which particular task I was doing, I would go and sit at a different desk pretending to be that person. In essence I was 'playing' a game of being a businessman. So one day I might be sitting next to the window as the Accounts Manager; looking after invoices, paying bills and keeping a close eye on the cash flow. The next morning I was perched at another desk, playing the role of Customer Services Executive; maintaining close relationships with existing clients, and managing their every whim to ensure that we were always the first choice the next time they wanted to buy. On other days I would be the Managing Director and then do my stint running the logistics department. Strange as it may sound, this became my methodology and my way of working, but the really important aspect of what I was doing in those early days is that I was documenting each task that each imaginary person who worked for me fulfilled. I was creating my own workflow and operational manuals for every single detail of every single job that needed to be done to make the business work efficiently. Each of these books had my complete philosophy and my beliefs underpinning them and represented a proven process that worked. So as I grew and started employing people to help run the business I simply handed them the manual and told them that is how they do their job. It was really very simple and it worked. Of course what gave me this way of doing things was part of my DNA due to the habit I had evolved through dancing, magic and cocktail flair. I needed a routine to produce a consistent, methodical and deliberate outcome.

One of the processes that I had worked out and documented was a sales methodology to win more work amongst the motor trade customers I was targeting. This started with sending out forty letters a week, had a structured follow up process of phone calls and visits supporting it, and even had scripted responses, suggestions and a close. This process was one that I handed on to the first sales people I employed, and one which led to SOLFAN becoming the national distributor for BodyMaster with several full-time staff and actual departments. By this time we were looking even further afield, outside of the motor trade, and developing products and solutions for insurance companies and the like.

By 1996 both BodyMaster and SOLFAN had grown significantly and we were duplicating so much that the obvious next move was to merge the two businesses together. So in September of that year I became a Director of BodyMaster with a financial arrangement which saw me earn 100% commission on every deal that I completed as an earn out. It was a real cash generator for me and provided a strong financial foundation alongside my growing personal reputation within the trade.

Getting my name out there as an expert was actually a designed strategy, probably picked up from being in sales for so many years where a personal referral is worth a hundred cold calls. I was very conscious that it wasn't what you knew, or even who you knew, but who knew you that counted the most. I was determined to be front of mind with the people in the industry that had the biggest influence. So my first flirtation with the world of self-promotion and high level networking included international trips to trade conferences, to be seen with and talk to the right people. At one point I even had a two-page PR article written about me in one of the industry's most widely read trade journals.

LESSON TO LEARN

There is a very important message here for business owners with an ambition to grow. You cannot do it by simply being good at what you do. Others need to know of you and understand what you can do for them; the old-fashioned English reserve of 'if they want me they will find me' just doesn't work. Although this episode in my story was happening during the 1990s, today's modern media means that 'being known' is even more critical than it was back then. The good news though, is that if you get yourself known by the right people, in the right places, in line with your business goals, then eventually the effect will become self-perpetuating, as the next part of my story demonstrates.

By June 1997 it seemed that our sales activity, our products and services, and the whole profile of the business had finally broken the surface and captured the attention of the big boys in the marketplace. They had clearly decided we were getting a bit too big for our boots, were making too much noise or were simply becoming a nuisance getting in the way of what they were trying to achieve. We were about to become the subject of a bidding war.

Richard, one of the founders of BodyMaster, was on holiday when a phone call came in from ADP, who even back then were a massive player in the IT Business Solutions market. They were requesting a meeting with the owners. So Simon, the other founder, and I attended the meeting and they put an offer of acquisition on the table. We agreed to wait until Richard returned to discuss the proposal. In the meantime another large business, Glass's Guide, asked to see us too. Simon was away for that meeting so I went with Richard and a similar offer was made. By this time we were starting to wonder if the industry knew something that we didn't, and this suspicion was confirmed when a call from a third interested party, PHH, another outsourced IT solutions giant, arrived at the table soon after. The three of us went to that meeting and the realisation that we had created something special slowly dawned on us. These three massive corporates (compared to us), who were all competing with each other, were now in a battle for our attention – and they had certainly got it.

So in December 1997 I found myself stepping into a role as Sales Director of the new BodyMaster division (now part of the Glass's Guide Group). From small time entrepreneur, to SME business owner and finally on to Senior Executive in a multi-million pound corporation in just ten years – without a single official business management qualification to my name.

Chapter 8

Millions become tens of millions and rescues are replaced by tragedy

Without really planning how I was going to get there, I had just executed an exit from the business that I had worked so hard to create. This gave me choice and opened the door to even more opportunities, in addition to which I had the security of previous success behind me, in both finance and knowledge. Neither was it just knowledge, like you might learn in a book; I had lived it, tried it, tested it and proved that the things I was doing should work in any given situation.

So at thirty-years-old, I was starting my exciting new corporate career, with a large salary, bonuses and share options – and I felt that the world was my oyster. Then, just a few months after the initial acquisition, I found myself part of a Management buyout, which saw Hicks Muse (one of the world's largest private equity groups) became the new owner of Glass's Guide. This made me a paper millionaire overnight as well as having a significant amount of cash in the bank. Business was going from strength to strength, life was great and the road ahead looked amazing.

My area within the new structure was car bodyshops and motor insurance, developing software products specifically for their marketplace and requirements. At the time the company was doing really well in the smaller contracts, with twenty sales people who were all performing and hitting their targets, but I was ambitious and there were bigger contracts out there for us to win. I needed a system that would take us there and that meant learning more about the one area of business that had eluded me up to that point. Bigger businesses meant more staff and more staff meant 'people management'. So I looked around for someone to learn from and educate me in what I would come to see as an essential foundation stone of the scale model.

There was a guy working as part of our team called Kelly Waters. He was amazing, having started his journey on a YTS (Youth Training Scheme) for an IT company, moving on to work for the local Council and then joining Glass's Guide. He was technically very competent, but also a brilliant manager of people. He had a real affinity with the company's staff at every level; what motivated them to work, what they were able to achieve, how they could be trained and developed, who showed real potential, and most of all how to get the best out of each individual. I learned a lot from Kelly. The combination of the work that I was able to do in systemising the business, supported by Kelly's expertise in building and managing a team of average people into one which delivered excellent results, meant that the growth soon became totally self-perpetuating. We had created a fully scalable, profitable and efficient business model which didn't require much more than an overseeing eye from either of us, and we had done it almost by accident.

LESSON TO LEARN

Once again there was a real coming-together of the principles that would eventually make up the scale philosophy, and this was undoubtedly the clearest example there had been of it up to that point. In Chapter 11, I will refer back to this chapter and invite you to uncover exactly what we did, but for now it is enough to know that the result meant I could be released from the day-to-day. Not just because my tasks were covered, but because there was a structure in place that allowed the business to scale without me. Remember scaling means something very different to merely growing because it is planned, robust, predictable and has an exit plan.

So Kelly and I sat in my office for days on end with our imagination and a whiteboard, and developed a concept called GlassWorks. In effect, this was an end-to-end process designed specifically to address the needs of the country's largest insurance companies and our customers wanted it. Having freed myself from the existing day-to-day business I was now able to experiment by starting again on my next, even more ambitious, project.

A few years before I joined the business, it had lost out in a bid for one of the largest and most important prospects in that industry, Zurich Insurance. So, with my newly acquired time, freedom, and my *Ad Astra* mind-set, I set out on a full three year project to make sure that when the tender came around again, we would win it. This was only possible because the day-to-day, 'bread and butter' business was being taken care of in a scalable, controlled way. It is really important to note that my job specification only required me to do the day-to-day, but because I had effectively exited myself from my business I was free to spend all of my time going after the dream client – a contract that would eventually be worth millions over a number of years. That is the awesome power of scale.

I approached the tender in exactly the same way that I had everything else in my business and personal life. It involved getting to know the people who were making the decisions and pretty much courting Zurich for three years. My initial goal, or Set up was: to make sure I fully understood their requirements; next I had to show them that I was aligned with their requirements by demonstrating that I understood;

from there I got involved in helping them to write their tender documentation (without them knowing this of course), learning lessons and implementing actions as we went. Finally, we came to the close.

It was July 2001, I had just got married to the lovely Jacki and I was about to set off on my honeymoon. That week I received phone calls from three of the main decision makers within Zurich wishing me and Jacki all the best. Now I had come to learn that the 'suits' do not communicate outside a tender process, it's just not the done thing. That was the point that I knew the project was a success. So when the final presentation of our proposal came around in the September of that year we were running the pitch as though the deal was done. Not 'cocky' but certainly with the confidence of having followed a system which was 'certain' to deliver. That is how I led the team which won Glass's Guide's biggest ever deal up to that time.

There is a saying which is applied to all walks of life that, 'all good things must come to an end'. Now, in the same way that I don't agree that success is ever purely down to luck, I don't necessarily believe that good things 'must come' to an end, but it is often the case that a spanner is thrown in the works when you least expect, or even deserve, it. That is what happened next; just as my perfect job and ideal environment was prospering so nicely.

A new guy was brought into the business hierarchy and given a position as my boss. Now I got on OK with him personally, and in fact we are still in contact to this day, but when it came to business we just didn't see eye to eye. It seemed that on every point we clashed. Maybe because I was from an entrepreneurial background and he had risen through the ranks of the corporate world where the survivors are political specialists, but it was clear that it wasn't going to work. This commercial incompatibility came to a head when I returned from a holiday in the Maldives to find his restructure plans had left me redundant. I can't blame him for this decision, I had seen enough to know that congruence in the management team was vital, but it was still a blow to my momentum. In fact, looking back at the experience it has helped me to empathise with other people who are facing redundancy and personal business difficulties.

This was not part of my overall strategy, although it did give me time to stop and reflect. I basically sat at home for four months (technically on garden leave) feeling a little bit sorry for myself and letting my mind wander from distraction to distraction. I watched the entire World Cup. I also did a little bit of gardening, even though our garden was smaller than a handkerchief, caught up on some reading and generally made a nuisance of myself around the house. As the longest four months of my life were coming to an end, I started to think about what I would do next (yes I know I should have

done this earlier but I am a last-minute person, remember).
A few ideas emerged, mostly along the lines of IT, software
and solutions, but I really wasn't excited or inspired by any
of them – then the phone call came. It was the day before my
garden leave finished when my old boss's boss called to say,
'We think we might have made a mistake – do you still need
a job.'

So I went back and tried to fit in with the new regime, and
to become the corporate animal that they wanted me to be.
But it just wasn't ever going to work, because I had scaled
myself into somebody that no longer slotted into that sort of
organisation – and there is another big lesson right there.

LESSON TO LEARN

It would be foolish to play Lionel Messi as a centre-back, ask
Michael McIntyre to anchor the BBC's news channel, or to expect
Gordon Ramsay to be a particularly patient waiter on the restaurant
floor. It is exactly the same in business. Whether you are trying to
make the most of your own abilities or those of your employees, it
is so much more than simply finding the right person for the right
job. To get the best from anyone and to manage their individual
scalability you need to match their skills (which are ever-changing),
their interests (at that specific stage of their career/life) and their
desire to engage with the company's bigger picture (which they
should, at the very least, be made aware of).

> Lionel Messi is too short to be a central-defender and his natural intuition is to get forward and score goals. Michael can barely speak a sentence without giggling or cracking a joke, because it is his nature, and the inappropriateness of Gordon's restaurant floor appointment needs no explanation! Any brilliant person, pushed into the wrong role will, ultimately, be a waste of time. Likewise, the right person in a role they have outgrown, or have lost their passion for, is a waste of talent.

After a few more years in the corporate world of unhappily trying to be someone I was not, I was offered the lifeline of trying to create a lifeline somewhere else. I'll tell you the story of how I was approached, even though it's not great for my credibility, to show how easy it is to miss what is right in front of you…

I received a call one day from Graham, a close colleague from elsewhere in the industry. Graham asked:

'Do you know anybody like you that might be looking for a new challenge?'

'Nope, let me have a think… '

A few weeks later another call from Graham:

'Any thoughts on that person, like *you*, who might be interested? It's heading up a new division.'

'Ummm no. Can't think of anyone. Let me make a few calls. Call me next week.'

A week later. Graham:

'Are you sure you don't know anybody like *Martin Norbury* looking for a new challenge?'

Ahhh! The penny dropped:

'Are you thinking of me?'

And that's how I moved on from Glass's.

It was a massive challenge, in many ways a crazy one, but it would give me a chance to apply the philosophies that I had been sub-consciously developing – on my terms. Once again I found myself in my element and once again the lessons that I had learned over the years emerged in the form of a strategy.

In April 2004, I started my new job as the Managing Director of a company that provided motor claims process services for insurers, a brand which was owned (and financially fed by) a global business process services and software provider. It operated as an intermediary between the insurance companies and the bodyshops; and it was wrestling with some seriously big financial challenges at the time. When I took over, the business was losing £3m gross, which equated to £250k per month. Not a great place to start, but music to my ears because I knew what confidence felt like, I had no fear of challenges, and I was used to finding better, more efficient ways of doing things.

During the three months garden leave leading up to April 2004, I prepared for my new role (I had started to learn that last-minute doesn't work at this level). I had no idea what I was going to find when I walked through the door, but I knew that if I didn't arrive with a plan of action from day one, then it would be impossible to get anyone else to buy into me, my potential, or my ideas.

The first stage of my Set up for this role was my appearance (and please believe me this was business not vanity). I realised that this was a major corporate challenge and I knew I had to look the part. So I turned up on my first day in my new luxury 4x4 car, wearing my new Rolex watch and new Oliver Sweeney shoes, with my Montblanc in my pocket and clothed in one of three Savile Row tailored suits that I'd ordered. It was very important that people knew I was serious.

I arrived with a ninety-day plan which went like this:

- Phase 1 – Thirty days of listening to everyone's point of view (customers, employees, suppliers and the market in general);
- Phase 2 – Thirty days of sitting down with the team that I had inherited, one-to-one or in groups, to discuss and create strategies for improvement;
- Phase 3 – Thirty days of implementation, communication and roll out of the strategies.

The first phase told me that our suppliers and customers were, let's say, not too fond of us, the employees didn't enjoy working for the company and there was a whole lot of wasted expense, activity and enthusiasm seeping through the business. It was also clear that the entire business was focused inwardly and completely stuck in the moment, with no vision or expectation that a way out could even be possible.

It became clear, during the second phase, that there was very little unity or congruency of vision within the organisation either. So we created a single goal – to make £1 of profit in a month – and shared this milestone throughout the business. I identified the people whose roles were critical to achieving this target, and whose heart looked willing enough to beat a little harder for it.

Starting with our humble, easy to understand and easy to identify £1 target, we worked backwards to recreate each individual's role around the tasks that need doing – not the ones that had previously existed. It was also important that they understood both the part that they played and what everyone else was doing to help reach the bigger picture. Then, once everyone knew what their 100% looked like and how that helped the cause, it was a case of implementation, ongoing measurement, correcting mistakes and becoming efficient.

The people who wanted to go or didn't want to play by my rules, went – and within a few months the remaining team were celebrating our first £1 of profit for several years. We had let the business find its own rhythm, put our feet in tune and in time with it, and then practiced and perfected until we had reached our goal. Just like a Cha-Cha-Cha. I would even go as far as to say that there were some difficult decisions we had to make, but once we had made them – it was actually quite easy.

LESSON TO LEARN

In one of the best business books I've ever read, *Alice in Wonderland* by Lewis Carroll, there is the famous scene where Alice meets the Cheshire Cat. Their conversation goes like this:

'Would you tell me, please, which way I ought to go from here?'
'That depends a good deal on where you want to get to,' said the Cat.
'I don't much care where… ,' said Alice.

'Then it doesn't matter which way you go,' said the Cat.
' …so long as I get *somewhere*,' Alice added as an explanation.
'Oh, you're sure to do that,' said the Cat, 'if you only walk long enough.'

Most businesses run this way – they are just going. Some are failing at everything, but even many of the ones that are making money, or maybe even growing and giving a reasonably good service – are just going, which means that they are in serious danger of falling down suddenly and very hard. You see, if a business has no visible 'guiding principle' or clear 'targeted destination' directing it, then every decision its owners make will be an emotional one, based on the short-sighted information at hand. If a business is being driven by its growth, instead of the business driving the growth, then it will always be vulnerable to what I've heard many accountants call 'growing broke'.

Within months we had completely turned the business around and continued to march on into even greater profitability from that time onwards. But much more than that, because the engine behind the process was a team of enthusiastic, engaged and congruently driven individuals, we also began stacking up awards by the armful. In just three years, the company had gone from a lossmaking starting position to being recognised as an award-winning business, and in 2007 almost all of the industry's National Awards came our way: from Accident Management Company of the Year through to Outstanding Achievement for Estimator

Accreditation, (a national scheme created to unify a disparate industry.

The success that we had achieved did not go unnoticed by our owners. Even the largest of organisations can hardly fail to recognise when a money vampire morphs into a cash cow into a star. So my next challenge was an equally exciting one – Duplication. Not only did they notice the reversal of losses into profits, they saw that it was process-driven; and they were smart enough to realise that it could be replicated. So we started looking for similar companies, acquired them and turned them around. Each time it was the same: we'd get the right people, set a goal, create the system, then manage, amend and perfect. Each new business we turned around a little bit quicker than the one before. So, over the next few years I enjoyed success after success within the Group, taking on new challenges, creating solutions, enjoying life at home and at work once more.

Things couldn't be better and when my wife, Jacki, fell pregnant at the end of 2009 I was looking forward to the prospect of entering an even more beautiful world that was going to be a whole new experience altogether.

Fatherhood was going to be the moment of my life to date.

On Friday 19th February 2010 my first daughter, Lou, was born… but she was born dead.

Part 4
Full Scale
Consciousness

Chapter 9

Finding my feet, my purpose and my strength

Forty days later, on Thursday the 1st April 2010 (nineteen years to the day of setting up my first business), I went back to the office for one day and then returned home, never to enter the world as an employee again.

The following day was the first Friday I didn't work.

I took the generous severance package agreed with the company, because nothing else mattered more to me at that time than to be with Jacki and try and make things better. I didn't really know how to do that, for the first time in my life I felt totally helpless and I knew of no process to deal with what we were going through, but I had to try.

Lou's legacy has become a big part of our lives. Remembering her is still tinged with unrelenting sadness, but it is not about lingering in the past. She is part of the reason that 'I don't work

Fridays' or at weekends. Those three days are family time and there is little negotiation over that – neither could there be because it is what we want for our time. My family is totally congruent with that goal and it is massively important to us. In fact, the simple act of implementing this commitment was one of the most significant elements of our whole healing process.

We had decided that we were going to drive the direction of our lives, and not let life drive us.

In reality, I couldn't just sit and wait for us to feel better. It was good to take some time out, which helped, but I soon realised that 'getting on' was part of the healing process too and I truly believe that it always is. So after a few months Jacki and I decided that we were just going to pull our strength together and get on – and that's what we did.

I didn't feel that I could get back into the corporate playground as an employee again, in fact I am pretty certain that road will remain closed now forever, but I needed to do something. Just as the IT marketplace had moved on massively since my early days fixing computers with a soldering iron and selling glorified calculators as software, so had my skill-set; and since I had decided that I no longer wanted to run businesses, but I felt sure I knew how to scale them, it was also clear to me that I needed to share what I knew. The next obstacle was that, while the international motor industry might have known who Martin Norbury was, no one else would have a clue – and nor would they care. So I needed a profile and an interested audience.

LESSON TO LEARN

One of the more curious observations that came to light during my early exploits running my own business and subsequent career in big business was that the corporate world needs more entrepreneurial spirit and the entrepreneurial world needs more corporate understanding.

In other words many small business owners are surprisingly ignorant about even the most basic, but critical, elements of running a business. Terms like cash flow, balance sheet, business plan, pipeline, targets and even profit are all too often left to chance. On the other hand, most corporate giants have forgotten what it is like to be human. To think on your feet, apply some common sense, take a calculated risk or approach a problem a little differently; often seems to be beyond their thinking.

It always amazed me that the larger the business I worked alongside became, including those with billion pound turnovers, the less their employees and customers appeared to matter; they were numbers on two sides of the business balance equation – cost and revenue. I often hear business owners today joke that it would be *so* much simpler if there were no customers or employees and I wonder if those latent feelings manifest themselves as they grow their businesses.

It was the culmination of these realisations that gave me my first clue about how to share what I knew. So I looked around to find an existing, tried and tested product (with an established reputation) which could become my vehicle for riding into the small business world. I found the answer in the USA in the form of LMI (Leadership Management International), which was set up in 1966 by Paul J Meyer, a brilliant business teacher and strategist. The system was well established around the world with a host of success stories and testimonials behind it – and it was a system that was proven to work. It was also totally aligned with my own ideas and helped to reaffirm that there was value hidden within my story and the lessons I had gleaned from it. My idea was to use various elements of the LMI programme as an introduction to small local businesses, so I could then get involved on a more personal level and help them deal with their growth and scale issues.

Alongside this I began to network within the local business community; applying my ninety-day plan principle all over again. I would listen to their problems, I would talk about the potential solutions, I would show them how to make things better and then help them to implement the advice. So combining the structure, teachings and credibility of the LMI system that I had bought into with my own experiences, I began to build a client base around the Thames Valley area where we were living.

The motor trade that I had been part of also wouldn't let me fester, while I was true to my self-made promise of not returning to corporate life, I could not ignore the many requests for board level support that I received. To facilitate this I set up a programme called Advocate. This was basically a process, which meant I could step into any business (initially it was motor trade companies) and act as their Chair for initially one year. During that time I would visit the owners four or five times a year, focus them, make them accountable, and then help them develop a route to success. This would be supported by regular phone calls and performance analyses, and would always be driven by their bigger goals. They would make the final decision about where they wanted to get to but I would advise, sometimes steer and always tell them the truth about their choices. It was very successful, and I even started to franchise the model to allow other experienced people to deliver the programme under the Advocate brand.

Having other people involved in my business has always been important for me, and I have yet to meet the business owner, entrepreneur or CEO who can do everything on their own. At least, I've come across a few that try, but have never met one that does to any level of success. In this I am no different.

You may recall that I started this book by saying that I am not much of a 'people person', but that I understand a lot about people. While reading, you may have wondered why I said that, because everything I have done has revolved around other people. To my mind a 'people person' is one who easily engages with others socially, enjoys their company in any environment and naturally builds rapport. When I need to, all of those things are within my capability (although I tend to hide behind flair), but I would rather be watching, learning and getting the measure of the environment. I recognise that people are the vital factor in any business, but it is the system which will get the best out of them. The system is the difference between a businesses which is being run haphazardly, with no direction and little more than hope to guide its sails, and a structured, planned, perfected and well-executed success model. For me, there needs to be a purpose to personal engagement, not just social chit-chat. Again, it is only now, looking back through the passage of time that I have really identified these things, and the reason that I mention them now is because 'knowing your own strengths' is a really important aspect of scaling your business.

LESSON TO LEARN

While floating across the dance floor, fuelled by hours of practice and commitment to the cause, my purpose was not Julie, it was the 8-to-10 Cha-Cha-Cha – and so was hers. Throughout my education, those around me inspired me to be different and ask questions, not to be socially acceptable. When I performed magic and cocktail flair it was not to make friends, but to win recognition of my abilities; a few moments in the limelight and maybe attract a girl or two. As I got into business I was driven, first by the lack of ambition in people around me, then by aspiration to achieve the success of others. As I moved from challenge to success and back to challenge I attached myself to those I could rely on and avoided those that were not playing my game. Today, there is always space in my life for those I love unconditionally, but when it comes to business, I only really have time for those that want my help and those that can help me share it.

I hope that doesn't make me sound like a one-dimensional person, but it is important for you to understand that some people will help you reach your goals, and others will hold you back. Some people have no aspiration to 'not work on Fridays' or to start a business, scale that business and then free themselves to go and do something fantastic with their lives. I assume, if you are reading this book, that you are not one of those people. I assume that you have ambitions, dreams and obstacles that are stopping you get there. Well people can either help you or hinder you. So be wise in choosing those that you bring into your business with you.

Talking of people to help you, I started networking with a guy called Chris, who had lots of management experience, a strong commercial background, had sold-up and was looking for new opportunities to fill his Fridays (Thursdays, Wednesdays, Tuesdays and Mondays). He fitted my description of a perfect future business partner, firstly because he understood me and the way I worked, and secondly because he was much more of a 'people person' than me. He got involved in the LMI program with me, initially as a client as I started to take on a few clients, teaching them everything from time management, through to business planning and leadership training. It was going well and the Advocate programme was also bringing in a good stream of new clients, but I still felt we were missing a trick within the small business sector. It was soon afterwards that I came across an organisation called The Entrepreneur's Circle (EC), run by a serial entrepreneur called Nigel Botterill, who has a big personality and an impressive track record. I subsequently joined Nigel's EC as a member and started to learn his methodologies around online marketing, copywriting, goal setting, success mentality and a host of other (slightly outside of the box) ideas.

I learned a lot about myself and other people in 2010 and thought that in 2011 things would level out. How wrong I was.

Chapter 10

The Emerald City and
what's really behind the curtain

By the time I joined the Entrepreneur's Circle it had been running for a few months and Nigel was thinking about scaling the business (a clear indication that we were going to get on) so he made an announcement. Jacki and I were on a trip to New York and the Caribbean when I saw the announcement from Nigel, which he did in an enticing and intriguing way, by inviting members to highly secretive meetings taking place all over the country, flavoured by the promise of some really exciting news. It was, quite simply, an irresistible temptation. So, in January 2011, I went along to the local Secret Squirrel meeting being held at the Madejski Stadium in Reading.

The Entrepreneur's Circle is a membership organisation, dedicated to teaching small business owners the things that they need to do to break away from the large pool of the average, and start swimming in the exclusive arena of the successful. At the time there were just a few hundred members from across the country, and it was becoming harder for Nigel to engage with the entire membership on a personal level. So, that evening he presented his plans to franchise the business model, with an invite to apply to become part of his team of BGAs (Business Growth Advisors). Not only was it an orchestra of opportunity to my ears, I was also very impressed at the application of a scale philosophy that I had just witnessed (although I still hadn't quite identified it as such at that point).

I spoke to Chris about the opportunity and he jumped at the chance. Our application sailed through and so Chris and I became the BGA (Business Growth Advisors) team for the Thames Valley area. After an intensive three day training course, where I got to know Nigel a lot better, we came away with a clear, concise and structured template on how he wanted us to build our membership. The plan was brilliantly compiled, laying out all of his experience but with plenty of room to blend in our own. As we went through the three days Nigel delivered his strategy: starting with his teams' experience; bringing in our thoughts, ideas and feedback; launching new ideas and reinforcing old ones; laying down rules and measurements; agreeing actions and introducing clear channels of communication and feedback. Back at our office in Camberley the following day, all we did was start to implement the things that we had spent the last three days interactively learning. It seemed like the only logical thing to do – it did to us at any rate.

So by April 2011 my business revolved around teaching, mentoring and most of all giving small business owners the power to focus on what they should be doing each day. It ran under a number of guises; Advocate, LMI, BGA, and working alongside other mentors, but essentially I had found something that I loved doing again. As far as EC went, we set ourselves a very clear goal: we created systems in line with what the training had taught us; we set up marketing pillars and sales pipelines; ran meetings and provided training; we measured the success of everything and improved each process as we went along; and we created a real buzz around the members within our area. That, of course, meant that the business was growing on all fronts and the more it grew, the more faith we had in the process, the more we were able to push it and the more success followed. It was scale in perpetual motion.

Importantly, I was still able to have every single Friday at home with my family!

We had a great year in the business; having set it up correctly, built a congruent team ethic, created alerts to measure the activity, listened to the lessons that the measurements told us, and allowing me the time to exit the business as and when

I needed to be at home. Not only was it a successful business model, in terms of providing job satisfaction and a fairly sizeable income; it also meant that I was in control of my own time – completely.

In early 2011, Jacki fell pregnant with twins, Lily and James, who were born in October. Two healthy, beautiful and much-loved bundles of life, who have provided even more inspiration and insight into why it is so important to get the balance right.

Fast-forward to the end of 2012 and we were gathered together in Solihull for the BGAs' end of year meeting where the fifty or so regions would be able to catch up and compare notes. Chris and I were among the nominations for the BGA area of the year, not just for having achieved the highest number of new members, but also for the support that we had given to others along the way. Of all the awards that I'd won prior to that moment, this was really special because the final vote would come from my peers, the other BGAs. All the nominees were asked to present an overview of how they had achieved their results, before the vote, and we were amazed at the feedback we received.

When it came to our turn we simply stood up and explained how we had opened up the work books from the original training event and implemented what was inside of them.

We didn't present anything new, we had no innovative or inspirational ideas to share, we simply described the system that everyone in that room had been taught and demonstrated how we had followed it. There were some tweaks along the way, as we tested and adapted, but there was no rocket science to shout about. Afterwards we were still quizzed by a number of our colleagues asking, 'Come on – what did you really do?'

LESSON TO LEARN

One of the things that I have found in business is that most people cannot accept that simple works. We live in a world dominated by innovation and inspired thinking, but often what is already there works better. As you will have seen during the pages of this book, I have worked on both sides of this equation, and this is what it has taught me. It is not a complicated lesson (the best ones rarely are) but it is an important principle in the scale philosophy.

1. Listen to the people that are already doing the job
2. If it works then measure it, improve it and learn from it
3. If a better way appears or a stand-out performer – then bring everything else in line with that

Then measure it, improve it and learn from it

There will always be new, but new does not always mean better.

We did not win the Business Growth Advisor of the Year award that year, but did the following year by again following the same process, routines that worked previously and then adding to it when we knew it was working as best it could. Shortly afterwards we were further recognised as the entire organisation's Entrepreneurs of the Month for the success of that and our other activities. By this time the EC had grown its membership to several thousand members, so our reputation was fairly well established and that set us up for the next stage in the scaling of our business.

One of the developments that I had seen Nigel create within EC was to set up Mastermind Groups for his most ambitious members. He would meet on a regular basis with those business owners who were really serious about business growth and were prepared to pay for his time (one-to-one and with the other mastermind members) to get guidance, accountability and support. It was both financially rewarding for Nigel and the results proved that, for most of those involved, it was also massively benefiting their businesses.

So while driving home from an event and discussing where we could go next, Chris and I hatched up a plan to create our own Mastermind Groups. They would be run as a joint venture, in partnership with Nigel and some of his senior team, and would be based around our geographic area. Once again the scale philosophy had enabled me to Set up a process; implement it, adjust and perfect it; then exit myself from it so that I could move on to bigger and more exciting things, like running our own Mastermind. By now, perhaps because I'd spent a few years looking at what I was doing through the eyes of a mentor teaching others, I was starting to actually understand how scaling worked.

Nigel loved the idea (it was scaling his business too, because we were growing his income and reputation at very little cost or time to him), so we set about creating a marketing plan. The delivery would be fairly straightforward here because we were simply duplicating the model that already existed and had given results. Such was the power of the EC brand and the reputation that we had garnered by our own personalities in association with it, that the selling really was quite easy. We were over-subscribed and eventually went on to set up several more groups. As business owners you hear of 'gurus' that have created million pound empires in a few years, well our first Mastermind from the 'let's do it, Chris' to closing the applications yielded a potential £161,000 for all involved in *two* weeks.

As is often the case when you hit on a system and a methodology that works, other people observe the results and decide they would like to have some of that for themselves. Before we knew it, we had become the flagship Mastermind model that many of the other BGAs were following. There were groups all over the country, led by some of the more successful BGAs in association with members of the senior EC management team. We were of course generous advocates of the initiative and gave as much help as we could, wherever we could.

As part of my role in leading the development of the wider BGA Mastermind model, I began attending some of the Mastermind Groups that Nigel ran himself with his most valued customers and it was during one of those meetings that I started to get real clarity about the potential of scale and just how powerful it could be. This was the moment described back in Chapter 2, when Kate Lester, another member of the group, turned to me and said, 'You are like my scalability coach.'

In that moment I started to join the dots and see the pattern. It took me forty years and a suggested interview about my life with Carole Aldred, another mastermind member, to see it. Hopefully it has only taken you the pages of this book, but if it hasn't completely sunk in yet let me spell it out for you in a moment, first let me recap on some of the principles.

We start off bringing everyone together with a vision – a goal that the business is looking to reach.

To achieve this initial vision the business needs to align everything and everyone (skills, behaviours and roles) to help deliver all aspects.

A business cannot just rely on finding the best people (a goal to be continually pursued however) so it also needs to align its processes, technology and knowledge to provide the best opportunity of delivering excellence but in a methodical, systemic and consistent basis.

As the business scales it needs to be confident that what it delivers is repeatable over and over again.

With the right people and processes comes the knowledge of how well both are doing in delivering the promise of the business, through moments of truth and key measurements from all stakeholders, as to how the business can consistently improve in all areas.

So based on the above summary my scale model is:

THE SCALE MODEL™

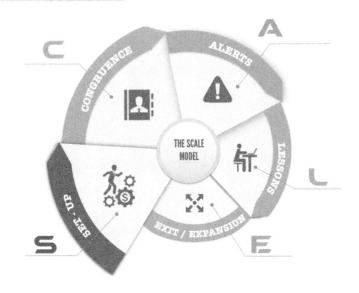

Set up: getting absolute clarity on exactly what the end goal is – and why it is so important

Congruence: ensuring that everything and everyone who needs to be involved understands their role (and the goal)

Alerts & Alarms: measuring the activity that creates the result and highlighting when it is not met

Lessons Learned: continuous improvement by noticing and correcting mistakes (i.e. anything less than 100%)

Experiment, Expansion or Exit: releasing your involvement and giving you freedom to do anything you want.

In the next chapter I will describe a few examples of the SCALE Model in action, as described earlier in this book. As you look at some of the summaries, it might be a good idea to re-read those sections and see if you can spot the clues as you read through them again.

Chapter 11

A look-back at SCALE
through its stages...

Now that I have revealed what the SCALE acronym stands for, let's go back and look at few of the examples that I described earlier in the book to see how it made all of the difference.

Although there were many elements of SCALE which I had stumbled upon, learned, or employed up to this point, it was when Kelly and I were running the Glass's Guide division that the first full SCALE model appeared. Go and read the short section again in Chapter 8 and then come back and look at the summary here:

Set up: Glass's Guide had set us some tough, but achievable sales targets – so we knew exactly what we needed to achieve. That meant we could design a process that would hit the right numbers efficiently. It included a comprehensive breakdown of each individual's role – what they did and what their own 100%

looked like. It mapped out how everyone interacted and worked together to fulfil their part in the bigger picture.

Congruence: There was a clear philosophy behind the detailed process that we had documented and implemented. Its purpose and drive were: consistently hitting sales targets, efficiently delivering products and maintaining excellent service and total satisfaction. Everyone understood that this was the goal and everyone enjoyed the results of achieving it together.

Alerts & Alarms: Because we knew what 100% looked like for the business, and for every individual operating within it, we were able to set up ways of monitoring the performance. Because of the **congruency** already established in the business, no one saw this as 'big brother' because everyone wanted the same result. This meant that I knew (with 99% certainty) on any given day what that month's sales targets would finish at. Activity delivers results in a rhythm.

Lessons Learned: Every time a target was missed the relevant person (usually a manager) looked at the situation and made an assessment. If it was a one-off or a blip in the system then it could be ignored, but if it happened again the situation would be addressed. This was done on a daily basis and meant that solutions could be developed or the process adapted to readdress the 100%. Again – everyone had already bought into the final goal, so everyone wanted the same thing – 100%.

Experiment, Expansion or Exit: As the managers of the SCALE model that we had created, we had effectively exited ourselves from the day to day operation, almost completely. All that was required of us, to keep the business running was to check the **Alarms & Alerts** each day. That meant we were free to look at other opportunities and for me that meant focusing on winning bigger contracts. The result was the multimillion deal with a large financial group, followed by two more in quick succession.

The next comprehensive example of SCALE that I shared with you was also in Chapter 8 when I took a large corporation from losing £250k per month into making its first pound and then into serious profit. Here is how the actions that I introduced match the scale model:

Set up: I described my 90-day plan at the start of the process in Chapter 8. The point of that exercise was initially to understand what was going on in the business and to see where the failings were. An important part of 'knowing where you are going' is 'knowing where you are now'. Once I had done that, the next important step was to create a detailed plan around how we would get to our first £1 of profit. Notice the use of the word *we* there.

Congruence: A major part of the **Set up** or plan involves the people who will be implementing it. That means that everyone in the business (the ones who remained in it) had to understand the bigger picture. They had to buy in to the goal, be **congruent** with it, and desire it. So when it came to identifying their part in the plan, their 100%, they would not see it as a chore, but as personal involvement in the overall success.

Alerts & Alarms: We had taken some pretty tough decisions to get the business in a place where it had the potential to make a profit. This meant some people leaving (the reality was that 'some' didn't want to be a part of the solution and 'all' would have paid the price if they hadn't left) and others had to come up to speed. So we owed it to the business and the people to measure their performance. This was not a stick to beat them with, but a ruler to help them reach their 100%. The key here is the willingness to do it, not the having to do it.

Lessons Learned: Whenever you set out to do something new, or introduce a new system of doing something you will always have to start with an element of guesswork or estimation around what 100% means. This was certainly the case here and part of the journey towards becoming more efficient was learning from mistakes and improving the process as we went. Because we had already established congruency amongst the team this was a surprisingly painless, but still fundamentally critical, process. Where a lot of businesses fail is they do not know the 'as is' to measure against to drive to that 100%, so it's a few steps forward but also a few back.

Experiment, Expansion or Exit: In this instance the result of implementing the SCALE model was not so that I could exit the business, because my initial end-goal was the same as everyone else's – to make £1. When we had achieved that target, we simply kept going, and continued to scale the business until it became a very profitable division within the Group. The unexpected, but for me really exciting, **'exit'** came in the shape of being involved in buying similar businesses and applying the same process there.

The final example of SCALE in practice is the story I covered in Chapter 9 which details how Chris and I took our BGA business to the top performing region in the country in 2012. This is important because it would be a mistake to have got this far and think that SCALE only works in larger business. On this occasion there were only two of us, but the same process was followed:

Set up: This was really easy, because we were given the plan during our three day training course. Where we later learned that many of the other BGAs (not all of them I hasten to add) went wrong was that their manuals simply went up on the shelf. This *huge* asset they had right in front of them, got ignored as they were searching for some kind of secret formula to success. For us they became the workbooks we went through (which were comprehensive and crammed full of wisdom and experience) and ultimately created the structure, upon which we were going to build our business.

Congruence: All that we needed to do was add out own personal goals, ambitions and commitments to the structure. What was really important, because there were only two of us, was that we understood each other's motivation for being involved. We needed to be clear, 'who' was responsible for 'what', and to both be fully in tune with the bigger picture. For example, Chris knew that, 'I don't work Fridays', and I knew that he had prior commitments to training for an Ironman endurance event. In addition, this was actually a part-time role for us and we both had other business interests independently. So getting the congruency of our goals right was vital to the harmony of our commitment.

Alerts & Alarms: Because much of what was involved in the structure, with which we had been presented was around the implementation of marketing systems, it was simply a case of setting up the process. Then we were able to press 'go' and watch the results come through. Once we had learned what should be happening we could easily look at the results each day or week and pick out any discrepancies. These became our **alerts**. The rest of the role involved teaching business owners the stuff that would help them to grow their businesses. And that was easy, too...

Lessons Learned: Of course, the original manual that we had been given was conceived in an office and developed in a classroom. That meant that, while it was brilliant (in fact I still refer to much of its wisdom today), some of the things we were taught worked better than others. In truth, some of it didn't work at all, but we tried everything we were taught, we measured everything we tried, and we learned what worked the best and what could be improved to make it work better.

↖↗
↙↘ Experiment, Expansion or Exit: My experience as a BGA, and even winning the awards that came as a result of it, were really quite small scale when you put it into perspective. By that time I had built up and sold a multi-staffed business from being a one-man-band, become a millionaire overnight, masterminded multi-million pound deals, rescued sinking divisions of global corporate giants, managed major acquisition projects... and dealt with the death of a child.

What the BGA experience did for me, perhaps more than any other, was give me a sense of purpose that meant I could finally identify both my 'why' and my 'how'. So, applying the SCALE model to my BGA business led me to finally understand the SCALE model in its entirety; and realise how I could use it to help other people. So I exited that too, and set about creating a model to bring it to people like you.

There are other examples of 'SCALE in action' in the book (in part or in full), many of which I'm sure you will have identified along the way, or now be able to see in retrospect. A few of the ones you might like to go and revisit include:

LESSON TO LEARN

Dancing in Chapter 3: As a young lad learning to dance, I started out with a goal that I wanted to achieve. I realised that I needed to employ systematic and disciplined practice in order to achieve the goal. This was my **Set up**. I was part of a team, so unless my partner had the same intent we were going to collectively fail. We were **congruent** with the bigger picture. Neither of us knew how to dance before we started, and certainly didn't know how to win a national competition. We needed experts to measure what we were practising; to **alert** us to our mistakes and ensure that we learned how to do things better. After we had won the 8-10 Cha-Cha-Cha we **exited** the dance floor with a massive prize (for us, our coaches, and our families) and were able to build on our success model to win even greater accolade.

Magic and Cocktail Flair in Chapter 5: Both of these things look like magic, and yet both are surprisingly simple, once you know the secret and have put in enough practice. For magic, in particular, the secrets are closely guarded but they are available to learn. Likewise with any type of flair or performance, you only need a little bit of natural spatial awareness to be able to learn to juggle gin bottles and cocktail shakers, but for both of these things you do need commitment, belief and a real drive and desire to get the end result. You can set up to be a performer by finding out the 'how to' from someone who knows the secrets. Your commitment must be **congruent** with your need to succeed. You will have to look in the mirror to **alert** yourself as to whether what you are doing is correct.

You will need to practice-check-practice-check-practice, over and over again until you have **learned** what perfect looks like. Only then can you perform to the crowd and take your applause as you **exit** the stage and hit the big time.

SOLFAN and beyond in Chapter 7: This was perhaps the start of SCALE in practice, albeit in its early development stages, as an unconscious process. I didn't really know where I was heading, but I did have a driver; which was that I understood that customers needed solutions, not products – and I wanted to deliver those needs. So that was my **Set up** and the purpose that I was trying to achieve. **Congruence** is the biggest learn that I can pick out of that story. The way that I documented the detail of every task I performed, to create my work manuals, meant that as I grew others could engage with my methodologies completely. Because I had manuals and processes in place, it was very easy to refer back to them (myself and later with my staff) to check that there were no alerts to address. I was totally naïve to business at the time; but I **learned** quickly and when I saw my mistake, I changed, amended or adapted the process accordingly. (Sadly – there are still so many business owners who don't do this.)

The rest of my story, the success that I have been blessed with, the way that I have been able to help others, and this book, are the result of the **expansion** I have enjoyed as a result of that experience.

In addition, I hope that you will have picked up a few more ideas, insights and education about the way to scale your business and perhaps about business in general, along the way. In my final chapter I have included excerpts from our clients on how SCALE has shaped their business growth, and one client that has massively changed their business by listening to an hour webinar of mine.

Part 5

Five simple steps to SCALE your business

Chapter 12
The FIVE themes of SCALE

S is for Set up

It seems like an obvious place to start to say you need a plan; and that is because the obvious truths are often the most powerful but neglected ones. In reality, this book and the entire SCALE model are about natural intuition being translated into a formal system. The reality is that most companies already have systems or ways of working (to varying levels of competence), but most simply do not follow them.

I mentioned earlier in the book the analogy from *Alice in Wonderland*, where Alice is asking directions from the Cheshire Cat, with the intention of just getting somewhere. Well most businesses are like that too. To plan well and understand how you are going to get your business to a place that you can call success you need to know what success looks like – for you. Some business owners might be aiming to build a massive business, sell-up and retire early; others want to create a healthy income doing the thing they love most in the world; and then there are the people who want to take over the world in their marketplace and go global. Whatever your dreams and aspirations, you will never, ever get there if you haven't nailed the goal. As the cat said to Alice, 'if you don't know where you are going – all roads will take you there.'

So to set up correctly or to start out in a way which will enable you to scale your way to success, you need to begin with the end in mind. Once you have your goal clearly identified, simply start to work backwards. Work out what your business will look like in terms of: finances, turnover, personnel, products, processes, structure and marketing. The word 'journey' is perhaps overused in our modern culture, but it is certainly relevant here.

Imagine you were driving to the shops. Would you make a plan? Not necessarily – but you would check you had your car keys, possibly take your 'bags for life', some money (or cards), and maybe even a shopping list. So there is a kind of rough plan involved. Short and sweet.

What if you were having a day out with the family? In that scenario you might take a map and plan a scenic route (or at least find the postcode for the SatNav). Maybe you would think about refreshments for the drive or plan a stop for lunch and fuel. If it was a place that you hadn't been before you would probably have researched the area to work out a few activities to make the most of your day.

How about when you go on a holiday abroad? That is a whole new board game. There are passports, tickets and foreign currency to consider. You would certainly have thought about transportation when you land, long before you took off. In all likelihood you would have gone there with a primary goal in mind: sun, sea, snow, adventure, sightseeing, exploration, relaxation or visiting friends. So you would have looked at all of the options to enhance these intentions. It would not be a light operation. There would be a plan.

Now consider how you would plan to emigrate to Australia? I think you get the picture...

The greater and more complex the goal, the more detailed the plan needs to be. If you have big aspirations for your business, especially if those plans involve employing other people, then you will fail if you do not have a clearly defined, step-by-step plan. The key thing here is what you do tomorrow will be fundamentally different in each of the above scenarios. You wouldn't take your passport to nip to the shops, the same as you would not just grab you keys and end up in Australia, unless a large amount of drink was involved.

When a company is small it is possible to run reasonably well without much planning, dealing with each new piece of work or challenge as it arrives and simply getting by. That is because the business only has short term goals. If you wanted it to expand, however, it would have to systemise or risk 'growing broke'. Haphazard processes simply aren't robust enough to cope with additional activity. The growth would only serve to amplify all of the problems or gaps in the existing model.

In order to grow efficiently (or in other words SCALE) a company must work out exactly what makes its business work and document the method. Consider this simplified example of our imaginary business, The Picnic Company.

1. The sales and marketing process (minimum performance required: fifty calls per day, resulting in three meetings, resulting in one new order)
2. The delivery of each new order (minimum performance required: the design needs a two-day turnaround, the production another two-day turnaround, and the delivery is the following day)
3. The invoicing and collection process (minimum performance required: send the invoice on the day of the order, then collect payment before releasing the goods for delivery)
4. The customer service process (minimum performance required: call within two days of

delivery, then arrange a visit within one week, resulting in 75% re-orders)

5. The follow up process (minimum performance required: add the 25% who didn't re-order to a mailing list, resulting in 10% of them re-ordering at a later date). The customer service team carries out this step.

Let's say that the process described above is the starting point which is delivering a turnover of £20k per month. You have now worked out the process and the performance targets that will guarantee you achieve that target (based on measuring your current success). If your goal is to turn £20k per month into £100k per month then all you need to do is work out what the numbers need to look like in order to achieve that clear and defined goal.

This could be achieved by employing more staff, training the existing ones to perform better or, most likely, a combination of the two. But because you have mapped out the entire process beforehand you can see exactly where the investment needs to be and avoid causing more strain than necessary on any particular area of the business. For example; simply increasing the sales performance without adding enough resource to manage the production will cause failures and only upset your existing clients.

It is so important to get the Set up or strategy in place, before you start to grow, in order to maintain the integrity of the business model. I am not suggesting, by any means, that you take all of the flair and innovation out of your business by making everything run in line with performance targets. You absolutely do not need to become a corporate, impersonal machine to be able to SCALE. You simply need a map and a very clear direction or you will never get to where you want to be.

'The corporate world needs more entrepreneurial spirit and the entrepreneurial world needs more corporate understanding'

The flair, fun, inclusivity and innovation comes from the next stage of the SCALE model – CONGRUENCE.

C is for CONGRUENCE

Do you remember in Chapter 8 where I described how I took a large corporation from losing £250k per month into making its £1 of profit? That goal was a perfect example of congruency. Every single member of my team passionately bought into the joint vision. They weren't simply doing their job, hitting the numbers or trying to achieve a target to avoid getting their knuckles rapped. They were involved in the destination at which we, as a unified team, were aiming to arrive. Everyone completely believed in the higher purpose and they were all inspired and excited by that version of success – not the job that they did.

Have you ever noticed the total unity of a F1 Grand Prix team? Every single member of the pit crew is dressed in the same outfit as the driver – complete with racing gloves and helmet. Between pit stops they sit together, huddled as one, as if in some imaginary cockpit alongside their driver; taking every turn with him and holding their breath as he accelerates along the home straight. When the driver emerges triumphantly into the winners area it is this team he 'high-fives' first, each one still clad head-to-toe as an exact replica of him. The looks on their faces and the delight emulating from their bodies easily equals that of the driver – it is as though they flew under the chequered flag at 200mph alongside him. The team's management looks at individual performances and measures absolutely everything to the finest degree, but ultimately the entire team 'wins together and loses together'.

In your business it is just the same, the alignment of the team and its clarity about the larger goal is vitally important. If you are simply setting targets and demanding more of your staff but they do not feel any connection with the business as a whole; their role is only ever going to be 'just a job'. Even sales people, or those in other roles where a bonus is paid for performance, will not be as engaged and focused on a simple 'target' as they would about a 'vision'.

Congruence involves developing a culture, which starts with you, as the business owner, and permeates throughout every level of the organisation. Whether you are a team of three, 300, or 3,000 it works the same way, although the larger the business the harder it is to maintain – it is also fair to say that the larger the workforce the more important this unity of vision is. Let's look at the same imaginary company we introduced in the Set up section:

At the beginning of the year you held a team meeting where you explained that one of your goals was to win the Supplier of the Year award. This would put the business in a position where the following year it could bid for some really exciting Entertainments Industry contracts and would probably mean 'free event tickets' and celebrity endorsements etc. With a young team in front of you, looking back excitedly, you feel confident that you've hit the right note and inspired them. During the rest of that week you jointly agree their new targets (referencing back to the big prize) and discover how each person's work affects the other departments' ability to meet theirs.

You follow this up by placing relevant celebrity posters and positive quotes around the office and a large wall chart to track the whole company's movement toward the goal.

1. The sales and marketing team: consists of two telesales and a field sales person, each with their own activity and conversion target. You have also agreed with the sales team that the two newly appointed apprentices in the delivery team need to be kept busy, or they might have to let one of them go!

2. The delivery team: consists of a designer, a machine operator and two new apprentices. It has been suggested to the apprentices that if they hit their targets they can go full-time next year. The two full-time staff have designed slightly lower targets to allow for training the new staff, but the team target is still a challenging one.

3. The finance team: consists of two people who, prior to the year start meeting, were operating on a seven day payment cycle. You have agreed that the new 'payment upfront' policy means that you can invest in new invoicing software at the start of the third quarter – this will make their role easier.

4. The customer service team looks after new customers and follows up those that didn't reorder: the department has one member of staff. You have jointly decided that there is an extra field sales role going – if the company wins the award. You have promised them that the job is theirs if they can increase retention to 80% and double the non-repeat order conversion rate.

By being open with your entire team, showing them how their roles integrate with each other's and sharing with them a company goal that they can engage with on an emotional level, you create unity. Then, when it comes to targets and measuring their individual performances, you are not serving out punishments but encouraging them to succeed. The mind set of enabling individuals to own their job and take responsibility for their role in the business is vital to creating a culture of congruence. It is about getting people to understand the correlation between them and the rest of the business, and how their activity and involvement impacts on the whole.

Having installed clarity and congruence into the midst of your team, it is now time to measure their performance to ensure that everything is working as it should be. To do this you need to set up some ALERTS.

A is for ALERTS

It is often said that a good manager is one who can delegate effectively, rather than feel that they need to do everything themselves. One of the keys to good management, therefore, must be having a team that you believe in and trust to do a good job. So if you have set up your system correctly and put the right people in the right roles with the right amount of motivation, direction and enthusiasm; all that you then need is a way of measuring the system.

The idea of having alerts or alarms operating within the business is that they are activated in real time. It amazes me that most business owners, even lots of really sizeable companies, do not know how they are performing until their accountant presents them with a set of year-end figures. Often this can be 12 to18 months later. How can you possibly deal with a problem that far in the past? My mind boggles at the thought.

The starting point for setting up alerts and alarms is to ensure that each member of staff knows what 100% looks like for them, in their role. This should not be a hardship or a 'ruling with a rod of iron' scenario, but simply an employee delivering exactly what is reasonably expected of them (100%) in return for 100% of their salary. A fair deal! When you add to this the precursor that they no longer see their role as merely a job, but as an important part of a joint vision which they have entered into, this is fairly straightforward. In fact they will appreciate the support.

Do you remember the story of my time at Wordplex, mending computers? My 100% was ten in three days, whereas the target was ten in five days. This was simply a case of a mis-definition of what 100% should have looked like. As I described in the full story, my manager missed an opportunity there, but with the appropriate alerts in place things could have worked a whole lot better. Missing an opportunity is one thing, but a far greater, often even fatal, offence would be to let underperformance go unnoticed.

If you have identified everybody's 100% and you set up real-time (preferably daily) measurements to check that the target is being achieved, then you can see if there is an issue before it becomes a problem. It might just be a blip or a bad day, that you can choose to ignore or monitor for a while, but if you 'don't know' then you are running blind. Things go wrong from time to time, the unexpected or unfortunate does happen, but if you have a robust system you can either work through it or make the necessary adjustments – instantly.

This isn't simply a case of watching the financials either. It is far more powerful than that. Let's go back to the imaginary company example we examined in the Set up and Congruence sections:

1. The sales and marketing team: the new, larger team, is now tasked with 150 calls per day, resulting in twelve meetings, resulting in five new orders (The Alarm: you know that if only 130 calls are made that you will not get your five orders and will miss your turnover target)

2. The delivery team: the new expanded team, with its apprentices and smoother operation, needs to deliver the right number of completed new products

(The Alarm: you know that your invoice team cannot ask for payment without having a delivery date – this will affect cash flow and hold up investment – so you need to identify early if there is a problem with the delivery targets)

3. The finance team: with a clear invoice and payment collection strategy, the team must be diligent about the process or they will adversely affect the cash flow (The Alarm: you need to be alerted early if the process is not adhered to because cash flow shortages have a knock-on effect across the entire business)

4. The customer service team: your service expert has to send enough marketing and make enough calls to deliver their new 80% repeat order target and double the orders from those who didn't order the first time (The Alarm: this will affect the whole new sales and ongoing revenue stream if it is not met – and mean that you cannot hit your turnover target)

In all of the scenarios above, you can set up systems to measure an individual's performance and alert you to any shortfalls – instantly. With that information to hand, you have the power to decide: if it is a problem, if you are going to let it run for a few days, if there are extenuating circumstances, or if you need to take immediate action. Without it you may be missing a massive pothole which could eventually destroy your business. Or you could simply wait for the missed targets, missed deliveries and lack of cash flow, then hold an inquest and make some redundancies.

Think of these measures as the dashboard of your car. You don't need to shine a torch into the petrol tank to visually see how much fuel you have – you look at the little dial in front of you. Likewise if a light comes on shaped like a bulb, it is likely that an indicator has stopped working, or worse still, one of your headlights. The warning light means you can go and investigate the problem. The alerts and alarms fitted to modern cars mean that you do not need to be an expert mechanic to identify what the problems are.

But here is the key point. The petrol and the lights on your car are all just playing their part in the delivery of the bigger picture. Each of the hundreds of functions in your car are all there for the same purpose – to aid you in getting you to the place that you are going, safely and comfortably. Some parts are more important than others at different times, in fact some are essential and others are mere luxuries, but they all have a role. Ignoring or removing vital measurements, like the petrol gauge, oil lights or tyre pressure alerts could cause you to arrive late – or not at all – ever.

That is why alerts are so important in your business. But they are also intrinsically linked to the actions which you take when the alarms go off. Let's talk about Lessons Learned next.

L is for LESSONS LEARNED

As I inferred in the previous section, mistakes are OK and not all mistakes and underperformances need to be jumped on instantly. While looking at the alerts that your system flags up, you are in a position to judge if there is a short-term reason for the alarm or if there is a problem that can be fixed.

Remember, because you are applying the alerts and lessons element of the SCALE model to people who already understand the Set up (or strategy) and have bought into the congruence of the bigger picture, they should welcome the result of a lesson learned. You are really looking out for places where 100% is not being met consistently and finding a way to make sure it is. There could be a whole range of solutions to the problems but the key is that you, as the owner or manager of the system, learn the lessons and take appropriate action.

Friction in business costs money in the same way that inefficiency does, so learning what causes these things is essential to being able to grow your business. A smoother running engine gives much greater performance. Likewise, if you were to invest more resources (employees, systems, or purchased turnover) in a business that is not running efficiently you would be amplifying the cracks that already exist. Often, rapid growth can be the thing that causes a business to break altogether.

Premature scaling can be the worst possible thing for a small business. It is best described as 'growing broke'. Either the business drives the growth, or the growth drives the business. Both might sound OK, but if you think carefully about these examples, in the context of the previous sections, you will see that the latter can be very dangerous and unstable. Let's apply the 'growth driving the business' scenario to our ongoing example, taking it from its starting position (as described in the Set up section):

1. The sales and marketing team were delivering 100 calls per day, resulting in ten enquiries, four meetings, resulting in one new order. But you then find a brilliant sales person who creates more calls, meetings and orders (this results in two to three new orders per week)
    Everyone celebrates this great new team member and the owners feel that the tide has turned in their favour, but no one thinks about SCALING the consequences.
2. The delivery team is now instantly under pressure, but perhaps there was some leeway in their

performance and they rise to the challenge (although the extra demand does initially bring the best out of them, ultimately they are consistently a little bit behind – and feeling the burden)

3. The finance team can only invoice on the day of an order, but with delivery dates being missed (increasingly frequently) they are missing their payment collection targets (this is causing some cash flow issues and some money-chasing letters to leave the office)

4. The customer service team is finding that many of their follow up calls are suddenly being met with a less friendly response; they are now dealing with late delivery issues, customers upset at payment request letters, and a few faulty product queries (consequently the automatic reorders drop to 60% and the follow up orders have trailed down to almost zero)

All of the above is the result of getting a really good sales person on board. It is the equivalent of putting rocket fuel in a Mini or a learner driver in a Ferrari. You will eventually 'grow broke', but if you are checking the alerts and alarms in your business regularly (preferably daily) then you can see where the potential problems are and learn the lessons they are telling you.

It may be that the system needs changing, that you need to employ more people to hit the targets, or that the employees need more training. Alternatively it might just be that the person doing the work has outgrown the position and needs a new challenge. Missing these sort of opportunities have caused many a star employee to go and find a new job with a competitor.

Learning lessons is an ongoing process, from day one through to today. Until you can look at your business and say, 'that it is perfect' or be absolutely confident it will continue to deliver the results that you want, there will always be room for improvement and always should. It doesn't have to be you doing the looking (as we will come on to in the next section) but someone must be continually improving it if you want to keep growing. Learning lessons is all about maximising the efficiency, delivery and profitability of the system.

As you continue to make amendments and adjustments to the system, by listening to the feedback that the alerts and lessons give you, the business will begin to drive the growth. This puts you in control and allows you to move on to the next stage of the SCALE model. In many ways the most exciting and fulfilling stage – The Exit.

E is for Exit, Experiment or Expansion

In reality this part of the model can represent a great many possibilities. Your goal could be to exit the business for retirement, a new challenge, because you have fallen out of love with the work, or because you have become a manager instead of a doer of your work. It can also free up your time to look at the next stage of expansion or experimentation for the business, without having to worry about the day to day work. Maybe you 'don't want to work on Fridays' anymore or you would simply like your evenings and weekends back to spend time with your family. Perhaps there is a hobby or a heart's desire that you have been putting off for too long and you can't wait any longer. Whatever the reasons you have for being in business in the first place, whether it is the love of the work or to create a great lifestyle for you and your family, being able to escape the clutches of business pressure is a wonderful destination.

In many ways the exit stage of the SCALE model is the natural progression for business owners that follow the process correctly. Being free to move on and focus on your goals is your reward for getting the system right.

There are many examples of this in my story and, if you look at your own story you will see them too. Consider how, when you finished school, you could choose to stop studying and get a job (based on the success of the lessons learned and your application at school). Alternatively, you could have chosen to take a route of further education (based on the same criteria). With each job you have taken on, you learned how to do it (the Set up), you engaged with it emotionally (congruence), you either performed well or badly (alerts), you either improved as you went on or went backwards (lessons), and ultimately you left the role (exit) to do something else. How well you did in the role, as you progressed through the various stages, will determine the nature, and speed, of the exit.

If your performance was good that exit may have been: promotion; you deciding to move on to something better; or you deciding that it wasn't for you at all. But it was the process which led to the exit opportunity. Where the lessons are not learned and the process breaks down, the exit may be accelerated and result in the sack or being pushed out. Likewise, I have learned that there are elements of the SCALE model (in full or in part) in every area of life and it is a powerful process when understood and followed.

SCALE is like the DNA within a business, and when it is healthy and fully operational, it can make any business grow effectively and efficiently.

Chapter 13

You'll never walk alone...
the Shankly story

If you are an Everton or Manchester United supporter, or you simply can't stand football, then I will almost forgive you for skipping this chapter. But even if you are one of the above, I would still urge you to bear with me because this is an amazing story and a stunning application of scaling an ordinary resource into a remarkable one.

Having grown up on a Slough council estate with an Arsenal supporter for a father (even though his family hailed from the north west) there was little reason for me to support Liverpool, but I did, and it was all because of the toss of a coin and the emergence of colour television. It was May 1971, I was just four-years-old and I had been sat down in front of the TV on FA Cup Final day. It was the early years that the Final had been broadcast in colour and as my Dad left the room he gave me strict instructions to cheer for the team in red. As it turned out there was clash of colours on the day, with both Arsenal and Liverpool's home kits predominantly in red. A coin was tossed which resulted in Arsenal donning their yellow and blue away strip. So instead of supporting the London club, as my father had intended, I spent the entire game cheering for Liverpool. As it turned out my misapplied favour didn't make any difference and Arsenal won the game 2-1, but that is how I became red for life.

The manager of Liverpool on the day that I started supporting them was Bill Shankly. Of course I had no idea who he was, or what a historic legacy he was building at the club at that time, but as the years rolled on I learned a lot about him. It is only now, looking back at the influences in my life, that I realise he was applying a kind of SCALE model too, and that is why his story has been included in this book.

On the Bill Shankly website the headline simply says, 'He made people happy'. When you read up about him and look at the man behind the legend it becomes clear that he was simply a good, honest, hard-working man, with a genuine desire to please the people he was working for and with: the fans, the players, and his management team (his Holy Trinity). That was his purpose, but it was not 'how' he went on to begin one of the greatest footballing dynasties of all time. The way that he did that was to create a system and install a belief in that system within the hearts and minds of everyone else involved in the club. History proves that he was successful in achieving that goal.

Shankly took over as the manager of Liverpool FC on Monday 14th December 1959. At the time they had been languishing in the Second Division for five years and showed no signs of achieving anything more that survival in that league for the foreseeable future. By all accounts Anfield was a sad place at that time in its history – a far cry from the song of confidence that would eventually become the sound of the Kop. The training ground was described by Shankly as 'a shambles' when he arrived and the low turnout on the terraces gave the ground no atmosphere at all. After his first game in charge he told the Board that the team were simply not good enough. He said that he had a squad full of average players, despite a few with some potential in the reserves and younger teams. The players had been walking alone, without guidance or vision for so long that it seemed that even the legions of loyal supporters had forgotten how to dream.

Bill's bigger picture was to turn Liverpool into the best club in England, so there were a number of milestones that he knew that he had to reach in his pursuit of this glamorous ambition. The first was getting promoted and following that he desperately wanted to win the FA Cup. With his objectives in place, he set out to build a structure that could achieve it. The results clearly needed to come on the pitch, but he knew that it was behind the scenes where the hard work and planning would have to start.

He assembled a team of talented backroom staff; people who were experts in the areas where was not so strong himself. This included other great names that would become long associated with the 'Liverpool way' such as, Bob Paisley, Joe Fagan and Reuben Bennett. Together they applied the philosophies that they had developed, operating from the tactical nerve centre of the club – the famous 'Boot Room'. Next he insisted on a complete overhaul of the club's 'Melwood' training facilities. After assessing the team at his disposal he quickly transfer-listed a full twenty-four players and set out to look for a handful of key replacements. This approach, along with many of the other initiatives introduced by Shankly, was quite revolutionary for its time and raised a few eyebrows both within and from outside of the club. Attention was then turned to what happened on the training ground and on match days themselves. There was certainly no room for anyone who didn't believe in the system or the ambition that Shankly was preaching. He was looking for congruency, and that meant finding his kind of people.

His game philosophy centred on what he called 'pass and move' football, which meant setting up practice routines to promote and perfect that style. This included the famous 'sweat box' ritual where a player would spend two minutes of intensely focusing on kicking a ball against a board, controlling the return and then bouncing it off of the next board. These sessions were timed and measured to ensure that the performance was up to the standard expected of each player. There was no slacking off allowed. He introduced ideas that were totally new to football, at the time, such as 'warming down' after exercise to significantly reduce injuries to players. Having disposed of the players that didn't want to play 'his way' Bill then went about recruiting for a small number of key positions and filling others with the talent that had been kept hidden away in the reserves.

Later, Shankly also set up a revolutionary scouting system to identify new players, which became the basis for the model followed by most modern clubs today. The depth and details of this scheme were rigorous but, like everything else that he implemented, the overall purpose was simple. The scouts were to identify if a potential player was able to 'pass and move' and also to judge whether,'… the lad had the heart to play for Liverpool.' These were the two most important features to look out for. Bill believed that methods and skills can be taught – but heart and desire comes from within.

From being an average team, surviving in an average league, Shankly's Liverpool finished third in the Second Division during its first two seasons. Then in 1962 the team won the division and were promoted. But that was just the start. Two years later, in 1964, the team was crowned as the First Division league champions (the best team in England) and the following year Shankly achieved one of his biggest dreams of winning the FA Cup. And much more was to follow...

During his fifteen years in charge at Anfield, Bill Shankly took an ordinary team, with no structure, no ambition and no future and turned them into world-beaters. By the time that he had retired from management his Liverpool team had won the Second Division title, three First Division titles, two FA Cups, four Charity Shields and one UEFA Cup. He had done it by setting-up an objective and then creating a system and culture that could achieve it. He shared this vision with everyone involved in the club to ensure they were congruent with his intentions. Shankly's ideas of congruency, unity and shared vision were exemplified in his decision to create the 'all red' kit that they wore at the 1971 Cup Final where I first bought into his vision. As with all good leaders, he wasn't averse to borrowing good ideas, and with this one he wanted to capture some of the famous 'all white' magic and togetherness of the great Real Madrid teams. He then created programmes and a playing philosophy, which was strictly taught, measured and adhered to on the training ground and on the pitch. His staff alerted him of any problems or players that were not up to standard and the lessons were learned (and where necessary dealt with).

Finally, and most importantly, in the bigger picture of the Shankly SCALE story, Bill exited the club and retired, but he didn't just leave a hole. He had started something amazing. The philosophy that he put in place has remained the foundation of the club from that day to this. During the rest of the 1970s and long into the 80s, under the lead of his lieutenants Paisley and Fagan, Shankly's Liverpool legacy went on to win everything and become the dominant force in both English and European football. The strength of the system that he installed was that eventually it didn't even need his presence to remain effective; and his successors reaped even more success from it than he did.

This meant that long after he retired, and even today long after his death, his legacy lives on in that he made his people (Liverpool supporters everywhere) happy. Shankly's great quotes about the game will live on long in the memory of Liverpool fans and indeed all appreciators of the beautiful game for eons to come:

'Some people believe football is a matter of life and death, I am very disappointed with that attitude. I can assure you it is much, much more important than that'.

'Football is a simple game based on the giving and taking of passes, of controlling the ball and of making yourself available to receive a pass. It is terribly simple.'

As you leave the dressing room and make your way through the players' tunnel to the hallowed turf belonging to Liverpool FC there is a plaque which Bill had placed above the entrance. It simply says, 'This is Anfield'.

Of this plaque, he said, 'It's there to remind our lads who they're playing for, and to remind the opposition who they're playing against.'

Chapter 14
What's your E-plan?

From the title and throughout the book I have made reference to 'I don't work Fridays'. I am sure you will have now realised that this is not about not working on Fridays or Mondays or any other day for that matter. The point is about choice and developing a business that provides you with freedom to do what you want. One of my favourite quotes is from Mark Twain. For me it was like a personal message with an actual instruction.

'The two most important days in your life are the day you are born and the day you find out why.'

I saw this not long after Jacki and I lost our Lou; it sent shivers down my spine and to this day still does. It took a tragedy at forty-two years of age to wake me up from my existence and start to find my *why*; to start to live the life I probably always wanted to, which went a long way to explain why I would work 14-hour days for somebody else. Yes, we had money and the so-called trappings of success, but I had no time to actually do anything with it. I had even convinced myself that I was doing this for Jacki and our future family; who was I kidding?

The really sad thing is that if Lou had survived I would have carried on with my journey, got caught up more in the corporate machine spending longer hours at work; looking for that next rung on the ladder; driving myself for what? The illusion was irrevocably shattered and so was my life, but then it started to rebuild and make sense.

As those who know me would confirm, I am a private person. It was a difficult journey for me to write this book and lay myself open, which I have done, sincerely, for you, the reader. I have *so* much respect for you; for anybody that wants to change their life for the better be it a change in career, starting up a business, or taking a risk based on the want, desire and search for their *why*. I have met hundreds, if not thousands, of people over the last five years who are like this but are struggling to find a way to achieve it. Some of you will have heard me speak about it on stage or through an article, maybe a training course or one-to-one.

I was unlucky and fortunate in that my tragedy forced me to look at life differently and re-evaluate what I was doing and *why* I was doing it. My wish for you is that you don't befall a tragedy like ours or any other that *forces* you to take action and be the success you are capable of and deserve, but by having read this *you* take action today, right now, and take that decision.

I firmly believe that my SCALE model works not for just for entrepreneurs and business owners, but for anybody looking to be successful based on their own definition of success. I have had discussions with multinational corporations, private individuals outside of their working life, government institutions, schools and even some of the world's leading business and information marketing gurus (we are all human at the end of the day).

While SCALE ended up as a business model I now fully understand and openly share the full range of tools and techniques that make up SCALE with my clients. Remember, it started out for an 8-year old with a dream of winning a trophy, a budding Tommy Cooper who just wanted to impress a few people and the young man behind the bar entertaining a crowd with a bit of cocktail flair and skill.

What about Joe and our deal from Chapter 1: did we get the £200 million pound backing to revolutionise the accident management and repair industry? No, we didn't, but it did happen for a large American private equity firm who purchased the company on 1st April 2015 for just over £43 million. This same firm has just agreed a £500 million deal to purchase the business I was CEO of (detailed in Chapter 8) where my primary goal was to make the company its first £1 profit. My reaction? A broad smile.

Chapter 15
The Hidden Idea

I was recently reading a fantastic book by a mentor of mine Daniel Priestley (and also who kindly penned this Foreword), and in it was this concept of the hidden chapter. His book *Oversubscribed* outlines how to take your business to a level where there is always a waiting list, and all the benefits that brings. The last chapter is entitled 'The chapter I wrestled with'. In it Daniel outlines that the story contained in one chapter was the one that did it for him, and he was a little scared to reveal it as the reader may undervalue it (you are going to have to read Daniel's book now!).

For me, outside the SCALE Model, there is one thing I did almost all the time to help me achieve my goals – but is not part of the SCALE Model. It is more succinct than that, and it is mentioned in numerous chapters. Like Daniel, I am not going to tell you, not because I am trying to be windswept and interesting, but more because on discovery it will mean more to you than me just telling you.

Acknowledgements

Cast of Stars

I want to recognise the people who have made *the* difference, they may not have known but they did at various points in my life. So, thank you.

Chapter 1   Kate Lester, Carole Alrdred

Chapter 3   Mum (June), Dad (Derek), Peter W, my sister Ches. Bill and Rose Phillips, Len Goodman, Julie Hills, Karen Bishop, Karen Moase, Samantha Campbell, Wendy Jones, Geoff Clapham, Michael and Vicky Barr, Sandy Smart, Sydney Francis

Chapter 5   Tommy Cooper, Tom Cruise, Andrew Ridgeley, PJ Harling, Beth Devonshire, Penny Woodcock, Mariana Crawley, Tara McNally, Barny North, Kate Hale, Penny Allsop Stuart Herd, Eric Wadsworth,

Special mention to Martin Gladdish, my book coach.

And to my Team of Swashbucklers past and present: Adam
Butler, Amanda Elliot, Andy Woods, Ash Taylor, Aynsley
Damery, Carole Aldred, Dave Lee, David Browne, David
D'Ambrosio, David Garcia-Gonzalez, David Laycock,
Glenn Ackroyd, Hazel Edwards, Ian Leslie, Ian Simms,
Jacqui Mann, Jamie Reeves, John Thompson, Judith
D'Ambrosio, Kate Lester, Keith Crockford, Mark Huggins,
Mark Rose, Mel Poynter, Mitch Lloyd, Nick Williams,
Nikki Shenton, Nigel Botterill, Sara Rose, Sian Nisbett,
Steve Briginshaw, Stuart Taylor, Stuart Webb, Terry
Gormley, Tim Edwards and Tom Perry

Clarry Kershaw, Peter Elsdon and Kevin Moriarty – my
rocks.

Jacki, Lily and James Norbury – my life.

And Louise Norbury RIP xx

The Author

Martin Norbury went from small-time entrepreneur to SME business owner and onto Senior Executive in a multi-million-pound corporation in just ten years. Setting up his first business in 1991, using a little bit of office space lent to him by some friends, he went on to successfully exit; years later he generated unbelievable results as CEO at a multinational corporation, turning a loss of £250k per month to celebrating its first £1 of profit in just a matter of months.

Back running his own company, Martin now helps business owners who are stuck in, or stuck on, their business sack themselves through making their business more valuable, more fun and even saleable. His SCALE Model is used across 30 industries, earning him the badge of *The Scalability Coach.*

A business turnaround specialist, Martin is actively involved in buying and selling SMEs, and advises companies on their exit strategies, how to leverage deals and maximise shareholder value.

As well as providing Non-Executive Director support for SMEs, Martin helps global giants focus on their business improvement through people development and effective personal management.

Martin has won a multitude of awards, including: Business Mentor of the Year 2015, Britain's Top 50 Business Adviser 2014, National Entrepreneur of the Month June 2013, and Business Growth Advisor of the Year 2012.

Martin is an approved Myers-Briggs Type Indicator® Qualified Practitioner, Fellow of the Institute of Coaching, and Fellow of the Chartered Management Institute.

Martin doesn't work Fridays!

www.myadvocatementor.com/books/
Follow us on twitter: @DontWork_Friday
Like us on Facebook: IDontWorkFridays

Printed in Great Britain
by Amazon

71449817R00098